Mechanization and Maize
Agriculture and the Politics of Technology Transfer in East Africa

THE POLITICAL ECONOMY OF INTERNATIONAL CHANGE
John Gerard Ruggie, General Editor

MECHANIZATION
AND
MAIZE

Agriculture and the Politics of Technology Transfer in East Africa

CONSTANCE G. ANTHONY

New York   COLUMBIA UNIVERSITY PRESS   *1988*

Library of Congress Cataloging-in-Publication Data

Anthony, Constance G.
  Mechanization and maize.

  (Political economy of international change)
  Includes bibliographies and index.
    1. Agricultural innovations—Africa, East.
  2. Agricultural innovations—Political aspects—Africa,
  East. 3. Agriculture—Africa, East—Technology transfer.
  4. Agriculture—Technology transfer—Political aspects—
  Africa, East. 5. Farm mechanization—Africa, East.
  6. Farm mechanization—Political aspects—Africa, East.
  7. Corn—Africa, East. 8. Corn—Political aspects—
  Africa, East. I. Title. II. Series.
  S494.5.I5A57   1988   338.1'09678   87-18258
  ISBN 0-231-06596-5

Columbia University Press
New York   Guildford, Surrey

Copyright © 1988 Columbia University Press
All rights reserved

Printed in the United States of America

For my friends on Hope Springs Farm,
Herb, Randy, Kate, and John

THE POLITICAL ECONOMY OF INTERNATIONAL CHANGE
John Gerard Ruggie, General editor

CONTENTS

ACKNOWLEDGMENTS

THIS WORK was a long time in coming and my debts are considerable. The gestation of the idea was a consequence of graduate study done at the University of California, Berkeley, with Jyoti Das Gupta, Ernst Haas, Carl Rosberg, and John Ruggie. All of these people were, in their own ways, tremendously supportive of the concept and the research. Haas and Rosberg were particularly generous with their comments on the thesis. Similarly, while the book was still a thesis, Ronnie Gruhn and Ben Schiff were kind enough to read and discuss various chapters with me. At the point at which the manuscript was prepared for publication, a number of colleagues and friends—David Deese, Don Hafner, Marvin Rintala, and Eliza Willis—helpfully commented upon and assessed a variety of chapters. Special thanks are due to Don Hafner and John Tierney who introduced me to the wonders of the Boston College Vax. In a very concrete respect this manuscript might never have been completed without their assistance.

My research was indirectly supported by the Rockefeller Foundation, through a grant held by Ernst Haas and John Ruggie while I was a graduate student. A grant from the Consortium for the Study of World Order allowed me to travel to Europe and Africa to examine the particulars of aid projects and programs. When I returned, both the consortium and a grant from the Institute of International Studies at Berkeley supported the writing of an early thesis draft. Boston College very generously invested in the preparation of the manuscript for publication with a summer research grant. And last, though certainly not least, the professionalism and good judgment of Kate Wittenberg, my editor at Columbia University Press, was greatly appreciated.

Perhaps my most important debts are to those technical experts who were willing to discuss with me the practical problems associated with international aid and technology development and transfer. Both national and international officials were unfailingly reflective about the endeavor in which they were engaged. All were concerned with the implications of my research for the improvements that might be made in international assistance. Unfortunately, my conclusions suggest that the necessary reforms must be be initiated by political, not technical, officials. There is certainly a great wealth of information and insight to be tapped in this community by Third World and industrial states.

The merit this work evidences is, thus, a consequence of a multitude of supports. The errors and inconsistencies are my own.

Abbreviations

CGIAR	Consultative Group on International Agricultural Research
CIAT	International Center of Tropical Agriculture
CIMMYT	International Maize and Wheat Improvement Center
CIP	International Potato Center
EAFFRO	East African Agriculture and Forestry Research Organization
FAO	Food and Agriculture Organization
IAEA	International Atomic Energy Agency
IBPGR	International Board for Plant Genetic Resources
IBRD	International Bank for Reconstruction and Development (World Bank)
ICARDA	International Center for Agricultural Research in Dry Areas
ICP	Industry Cooperative Program (FAO)
ICRISAT	International Crops Research Institute for the Semi-Arid Tropics
IDA	International Development Agency (World Bank)
IDRC	International Development Research Center (Canada)
IFPRI	International Food Policy Research Institute (CGIAR)
IITA	International Institute of Tropical Agriculture
ILCA	International Livestock Center for Africa
ILO	International Labor Organization

ILRAD	International Laboratory for Research on Animal Diseases
IMF	International Monetary Fund
IRRI	International Rice Research Institute
ISNAR	International Service for National Agricultural Research (CGIAR)
ITDG	Intermediate Technology Development Group
MADO	Masai Agricultural Development Organization
MOA	Ministry of Agriculture (Kenya, Tanzania)
NDCA	National Development Credit Agency
OECD	Organization for Economic Cooperation and Development
PWB	*Programme of Work and Budget*
SRDP	Special Rural Development Program
TAC	Technical Advisory Committee (CGIAR)
TAMTU	Tanzanian Agricultural Machinery Testing Unit
TANU	Tanzanian African National Union
SIDA	Swedish International Development Agency
THS	Tractor Hire Service
UNDP	United Nations Development Program
UNRISD	United Nations Research Institute for Social Development
USAID	United States Agency for International Development
WARDA	West African Rice Development Association
WEP	World Employment Program (ILO)
WHO	World Health Organization
WOF	*The Work of the FAO*

CHAPTER **I**

THE POLITICS OF
TECHNOLOGY DEVELOPMENT AND
TRANSFER

TECHNOLOGY IS POWER. Massive, sustained technological revolutions have internationalized commerce, reorganized agriculture, industrialized production, and given to contemporary society the new economic and institutional capabilities needed to sustain the process we know today as modernization. The sweeping nature of the changes with which modern technology has been associated explains in considerable measure why, despite disappointments and development setbacks, the Third World remains interested in the transfer of technology from the North to the South. Technology has not yet delivered the development cornucopia awaited by many in the Third World, but it is still widely identified as the resource most capable of transforming the basic structure of underdevelopment.

For better or worse, however, the power of technology is being interjected into processes of economic development in the Third World by political actors whose agenda for action is much broader and more complex than the technical mandates of the programs they support might suggest. The Third World state is the most prominent of these actors, but a multiplicity of international institutions participate as well. This has been perhaps especially the case in Africa. Colonialism left a legacy of scarce technological resources and extensive economic underdevelopment. At independence there were no technical capabilities available in the private sector—no group of highly educated technocrats, no middle class with the resources to invest in innovation, and very few institutions of higher learning and research with the ability to generate the knowledge necessary to support technological development. While the new African state also had very little technical expertise, capital, or institutional capabilities in an absolute sense, relative to other internal, private actors and institutions, it had more. And, as importantly, it was the focal point for the investments of international aid agencies. International assistance had access to the technical resources necessary for African agricultural development, and on the eve of African independence offered to the new state the programs upon which national development efforts would depend.

This investigation presents an assessment of the impact of politics upon the development, diffusion, and adoption of new technology; the impact of technology upon the political institutions that develop and introduce it; and the way in which states and international organizations interact politically through the joint execution of technology projects. The theoretical focus of the study revolves around the interaction of technical and political forces, the major assumption being that to understand the importance of one, the other must also be considered. The empirical focus addresses the attempts of two East African states—Kenya and Tanzania—to integrate new agricultural technologies into peasant production via the resources of international assistance agencies. These countries are among the poorest in the Third World today, but they are also among those African states that have most vigorously attempted to develop their agricultural sectors.

Politics as a determinant of technical innovation and change has been little studied and generally undervalued. Both the African state and the international agencies that assist it in programs of technical change are primarily concerned with establishing their institutional authority. Neither is secure in its relationship to the larger social, economic, and political environment. One confronts a social order of great ethnic and economic heterogeneity, considerable poverty, and weak institutions. The other contends with an international system of halfheartedly committed states, ruthlessly competitive organizations, and small budgets. Neither can afford to be institutionally self-abnegating. The very fact of the necessity of state building in Africa and organizational expansion in the development assistance community goes a long way toward explaining the nature of technology transfer in Africa.

More importantly, this challenge of establishing permanent, stable institutions while carrying out programs of technology development and diffusion has been taken up by both organizations and states in markedly different ways. Kenya and Tanzania represent sharply contrasting approaches to the problems of political and economic development in Africa—one capitalist, the other socialist. Similarly, in some areas of international assistance, agencies have chosen to pursue a route of traditional multilateral aid; in others they have formed new international regimes. The choice of strategies in both instances—states and agencies—is indicative of how institutions define their constituencies of support and how ambitious an agenda of social and economic change they set themselves. These choices define the context for institutional development and for how technology will be developed and diffused. Most important of all, some ways of establishing the state or creating international institutions work better than others to facilitate technical change.

Technology is a powerful development resource, and while it can be subdued to political imperatives, it also makes many demands upon its environment for support and sustenance. This necessity of providing technology with certain requirements of development and adoption make it an independent as well as a dependent factor of analysis. The institutions that develop and diffuse technical resources ignore these technical requirements at the peril of undermining the important economic impacts of technical innovation. At the same time, because technology is such a powerful instrument of economic development, it offers political institutions a larger array of capabilities in respect to social transformation and institutional development.

As in the case of political institutions, what becomes particularly interesting about the power of technology is its highly discrete character. The independent power of technology to determine the success and failure of innovation and to structure the social and institutional environment of its development or introduction varies considerably depending upon a host of specific technical characteristics. The development of high-yielding varieties of maize and the introduction of tractors and other forms of agricultural mechanization made distinctively different demands for technical support and presented institutions with very different capabilities for greater social or political change. Thus, some technologies make better instruments for state bulding or organizational development than others.

Finally, this book is also about the nature of development assistance. International assistance is most frequently studied from the standpoint of internal organizational politics and the development of the United Nations and Bretton Woods systems. When the implementation of projects is considered, it is done without full consideration of the national and international context in which the individual projects were themselves conceived and carried out. In the coming chapters I will trace the evolution of individual technology projects in order to reveal the way in which international institutional strategies of development overlap and interact with those on the national level. Understanding this relationship is crucial to a complete assessment of how assistance projects are actually born and how they grow to maturity, as well as to a full appreciation of where and why technology is successfully or unsuccessfully adopted.

The questions that will orient the assessment offered in the coming chapters embrace a duality of focus—politics and technology—as well as a concern with how the development assistance system as whole functions. Thus, in respect to politics as a determinant of technical change, I am interested in knowing when politics is an impediment to the successful development or adoption of new technology and when it is a facilitator; how particular state-building strategies or modes of international assistance organization result in different technological consequences; whether one actor as a manager of technological goods and services is more political than another. In respect to technology as a determinant of social and political change, I am interested in assessing when technology is able to impose its own design upon the society, the economy, and the institutions that utilize it; whether there are some technologies that are inherently more political than others; and how the particular characteristics of individual technologies inhibit or accelerate the objectives institutions pursue. And finally, in considering the nature of development assistance, I will assess when the state is able to subordinate the goals of international agencies to its own; when international aid agencies are most likely to prevail; and which kind of relationship between agencies and states most frequently accomplishes successful development assistance projects.

In this chapter I will locate agricultural technology in its system of technical support, and political institutions in their systems of social support. The power of technology to transform traditional economies and the power of political actors to establish their authority are both dependent upon the creation of environments receptive to their presence. It is, in fact, at the nexus of these two support systems that political actors carry out their fiercest battles with technological power, and that technology's constituency is defined.

Technology and Its System of Support

Technology offers African states and international agencies the power of economic development and resource creation, and thus the ability to accomplish many of the political as well as economic goals they set for themselves. But what kind of power is this? Is it an unqualified promise of greater wealth and welfare or are there strings attached, which as they are unraveled, reveal greater complexity? In respect to agricultural technology, there is considerable disagreement about this.

The most far-reaching technical change to have taken place in Third World agriculture has been the Green Revolution. The technology at issue is high-yielding varieties of important food crops—wheat, rice, and maize—but accompanying this technical innovation has been the adoption of modern chemical and mechanical technology. The debate on the Green Revolution is fundamentally concerned with questions of technological power. First, what kind of power does the technology exercise? Is it primarily technical and economic, or does it embrace social as well as economic organization? Second, to whose interests does technology speak? Does it act in the interests of society as a whole, or is it confined to more narrowly defined interest groups? And finally, is technology an entirely independent agent of economic or social change, or is it dependent upon other actors and forces? Those who celebrate the production successes of the new technology give very different answers to these questions than do those who are concerned with wider social and economic impacts. The crux of the argument, however, revolves around a major disagreement about technical systems of support.

The promoters of the Green Revolution identify the new technology as an extremely powerful agent of technical and economic development, a vehicle for the modernization of agriculture and thus for social progress and the interests of society as a whole.[1] Basically, the Third World farmer is seen to be an extremely efficient producer who knows very well how to allocate the scarce resources at his disposal.[2] The rate of return on the investment of resources in Third World agriculture is so low, according to this argument, not because of an error on the part of the peasant cultivator, but because the resources available to him are not capable of generating greater agricultural surplus. Thus, the productivity problem with which the farmer struggles can only be solved with the addition to or improvement of the resources upon which he depends. Enter the development of improved and high-yielding varieties of new food crops and other technologies.

A great faith in farmer rationality and technical power is mirrored in the writings of all Green Revolutionaries, but they differ among themselves on the role they assign to other social forces. The establishment of technical institutions, agricultural research stations and agricultural extension that develop and distribute the new technology, would be most effectively triggered, according to one group of Green Revolution theorists, in response to a strong market demand for such services.[3] Given the circumstances within which Third World farmers operate, such a demand can be triggered if factor and product prices—the price of the resources in which the farmer invests and the price of food—reflect the real constraints and capabilities of the nation's agricultural economy.

A second group of Green Revolutionaries are not quite so certain that the market can perform these wonders on its own.[4] While not openly criticizing their predecessors, these commentators assume that the technology will be most effectively developed and diffused if public institutions self-consciously pursue a policy of technical development and extend the required economic supports to farmers who need them. They have less faith in the market but no less faith in the technology. As a consequence, they are more explicit about the programs and services institutions must create or facilitate to establish the context most conducive to technological revolution. Beyond the founding of effective research and extension, they suggest that new agricultural industries, adequate transport, technical education and farmer training, accessible credit and crop insurance, and other forms of economic and technical infrastructure be created to propel a genuine and extensive agricultural revolution. They are, in particular, concerned that if the technology were to reach only a few farmers, the overall structural transformation of Third World agrarian economies would be delayed. Such encapsulated technical change would impair the ability of Third World agriculture to keep up with population growth and would limit the increase in economic welfare for which the new technology is responsible.

Critics of the Green Revolution, in contrast to the defenders and promoters of the technology, find that the power of the technology is not primarily technical and economic; that it is not acting in the interests of the society as a whole; and that, in many cases, its impact is controlled by other actors and forces.[5] Two primary explanations are offered for this pattern of social and economic development—one that concerns the nature of the technology, and one that investigates the nature of the society.

The technology itself is seen as a mixed blessing. The high-yielding varieties of Third World food crops, which are relatively inexpensive, are identified as a resource potentially available to a large number of peasant cultivators. They do not require sophisticated technical expertise and can be broken into a variety of units for sale and distribution. But, in many of the regions in which these seeds have been adopted, so have a number of other supportive technical inputs—from fertilizer to tractors, pesticides to irrigation—which are not quite as accessible to the small-scale landholder. This raises the cost of technical innovation considerably. In the case of irrigation the technology places the possibility of technical change entirely out of the range of poor, dry-land farmers, and in the case of both mechanization and irrigation, beyond the average small-scale cultivator.[6] In other words, for the richer and larger-scale farmer, the support base exists in the form of capital and a better infrastructure. For the poor farmer these supports are nonexistent, and technologies like tractors, if necessary for the cultivation of new varieties, make the entire technological package unrealistic.

Other critics emphasize that it is not the technology per se that is the source of the welfare problem, but social and economic relations that were already in place:

In analyzing the social and economic problems that have been associated with the spread of the new technology thus far, and which are discussed in this report, it is important to bear in mind that they are not inherent in the technology as such. Rather, they are the consequence of social imbalances and economic disparities that already exist, and are largely due to the fact that social policy and reform have not kept pace with the spread of the new technology.[7]

There is, in fact, a general consensus among critics of the new technology that inequities in the availability of land and capital channeled technical innovation into the hands of large- and medium-scale farmers, while missing small-scale landholders and the landless. Some peasants are unable, not unwilling, to adopt the new technology, because of their relative status in respect to other very important economic resources.

While in one respect the two sides of this debate are talking past one another—one group is more concerned with the policy mechanics of how to transfer the technology, the other with the potential impact—in another very important respect, they are walking around and puzzling about the same problem. Both sides implicitly agree that the power of technology development and transfer is a power that is highly contingent upon the existence of a requisite system of technical support. They disagree on which components of this system are most essential and why this is the case. In other words, some see considerable strings attached to the technical good itself and great complexity in the system of support, and others consider it to be a much simpler matter than this. The most optimistic are those defenders of the technology who argue that if markets operate properly, the technology will be a success and welfare secured. However, in fact, they are able to argue for a relatively small investment in the creation of a technical support system, because they do not believe that it is possible to orchestrate massive technological revolution. One simply cannot control, or provide for, all the necessary systemic supports. To quote from the work of one distinguished analyst, Yujiro Hayami;

> It is a gigantic task to assist millions of peasants in traditional agriculture toward sustained growth in their resource productivity. Adequate technologies that are different for different ecological and factor-endowment conditions have to be developed. Needed inputs must be made available to the millions at the right time and place. Physical infrastructure must be publically provided for, since small farmers are unable to procure it individually.[8]

Hayami is not certain that the creation of large-scale systems of support for small-scale holders will work—not, at least, in the short run. So, he lives with the fact that for the time being a small elite will benefit from the technology's introduction. In contrast, an equally prominent critic of the technology believes that such programs must be carried out (and by implication can be), if technical innovation is to reach beyond a small elite in Third World societies. Keith Griffin suggests the following:

> Once all cultivators are given equal access to the means of production, inequality will diminish and output probably will increase, the trend toward the destruction of the peasantry and the polarization of the community into two social classes will be retarded, and a foundation will have been laid on which a participatory democracy can be built.[9]

For Griffin what is problematic is quite different. To avoid the social costs of a limited program of technology development and diffusion, a massive program of technology diffusion must be attempted.

Thus, technical innovation is not simply a matter of the technology itself, but of all of those supports and services that result in its creation and successful diffusion. Markets, research, transport, land tenure, ecology, scale of production, and the like control whether or not the technology will succeed. Or, to put it another way, technology makes demands upon its environment as well as making promises to the actors who utilize it. If those demands are not met, the promises are not kept. If you are unconcerned about broad diffusion, you need not make extensive investments in technical supports. Both promises and demands are quite limited. If you wish, on the other hand, to reach the average peasant cultivator, you confront a very problematic cart-before-the-horse situation. Many things must be done at once; development must be highly integrated; and the resources at your disposal must be considerable.

In the coming chapters we will be concerned with the ways in which technical support systems—both broadly and narrowly defined—interact with the goals and capabilities of political institutions. Neither critics nor defenders of Green Revolution technology investigate the character of politics directly. Critics theorize about the state from their understanding of social structure, defenders from their understanding of technical and economic policy. Thus, for one group the state has no real autonomy from the society that surrounds it, and for the other it is a highly apolitical, antiseptic agent of development, characterized by the overwhelming importance of technical issues and problems. Neither considers the role of international assistance agencies, which was and is substantial. One of the most important ways in which the interpretation offered here differs from the literature on agricultural technology and development is the independent role I ascribe to political institutions. In investigating that role we will discover how state and organizational strategies of elitist or egalitarian development interact with technology's need for greater or lesser support. However, to fully investigate that role and to consider how technology itself may have an independent impact on both its own success and that of the political institutions that manage it, we need to adopt from the Green Revolution debate the issue that is most difficult to resolve—the character of technical support.

The three components of the system of technical support that are the most necessary for successful technology transfer are the organization of farm production, the technical and economic infrastructure, and the physical environment.[10] While every technology needs some variety of support from each of these components, the resources necessary from each and the particular interaction among them varies considerably. This variance sets the terms upon which an individual technology can succeed in revolutionizing production, as well as the terms upon which it may fail to do so. It also determines the types of social and political change for which the technology may be responsible.

The organization of the individual African farm embodies specific factors of production which include the availability of capital, labor, technology, and technical expertise. The limits imposed on technical innovation by the facts of individual farming systems can be considerable. In Africa, the resource scarcity of the majority of peasant farms means that while new technology may be capable of enhancing the overall resource endowments, there may indeed be too few resources to support its introduction. For example, tractors will always be capital-intensive. The average cost of a new tractor was under $10,000 in the 1960s, around $12,000 in the 1970s, and over $50,000 in the 1980s. The average African farmer will, for some time to come, be earning only a fraction of this. The average income in Africa in the 1960s was under $200 a year and has not increased dramatically since then. This means that if the market were to govern the introduction of the tractor, it would not reach most African cultivators. But despite these brute statistics, the availability of technical and economic infrastructure, can, in many cases, remedy this critical situation.

The technical and economic infrastructure comprises the public and private services that support agricultural production but that stand outside the individual farming system. This includes, on the technical side, agricultural research, agricultural colleges and universities, agricultural extension, and technical maintenance and repair facilities, and on the economic side, transport and communication, storage and processing, merchants, markets, credit, and national policies on agricultural pricing. If the regional infrastructure is strong—good transport, many merchants and markets, good agricultural extension—and the government is attentive to the need for credit and good prices, the limits imposed on individual farming systems are less constraining. But if there is little in the way of farm credit available, no local agricultural extension capability, low prices for farmers' crops, poor storage, poor transport, and few markets, the introduction of new technology stands very little chance of success with farmers who are resource poor. In other words, technology transfer is facilitated by higher levels of economic and institutional development and is constrained by economic and institutional underdevelopment. In regions of sharp economic underdevelopment or in situations in which individual farmers face serious resource constraints, it is public institutions that make the difference.

The final component of this system of technical support is the physical environment. This is a very different determinant of technology transfer, but one that is extremely important in agriculture. Soil structure and nutrients, bush and vegetation, the terrain, predators and pests, average annual precipitation, daily sunlight, temperature, and other ecological factors are all of potential importance to the success of the adoption of new technology. For example, high-yielding and improved varieties of maize are very dependent upon ecological circumstances. The technology is developed in respect to particular rain, light, and temperature regimes, and when adopted outside of the particular ecological zone to which it is attuned, the technology cannot perform with the same effectiveness, if at all. Just as capital-intensive technology makes it easier for political institutions to meet the needs of larger-scale farmers, the ecological biases of technology present them with the possibility of reaching some regions—and thus some ethnic communities or classes of farmers—before others.

Technology development, in contrast to technology transfer, is a better understood and less complex social and economic process. That is not to say that the scientists and technicians engaged in technical research can always predict the outcome of their work. There is an important element of serendipity to both basic and practical research which defies systematization and orderly progress. But there is agreement on what circumstances support research breakthroughs and productive science, and it is not a matter of orchestrating many interactive, mutually dependent components of success as is the case in technology transfer.

Technology development is very much dependent upon the creation of a cadre of well-educated and well-trained scientists and an organizational environment in which they can freely interact and work.[11] Unlike pure research, upon which much technology development is based, technical research is oriented to practical technical or economic goals. Technology is invented or improved to cut labor or capital costs, to save time and thus expense, and to increase output and thus revenue. In this way, productive technology development is also dependent upon an institution, private or public, setting a practical agenda to which science addresses itself. The market—national or international—may trigger this institutional actor, or the choice to create a research capability may respond to independent social and political forces. Whichever is the case, there is general accord on the fact that beyond the practical agenda, researchers should be given the freedom and the security to explore, reflect, reassess, create, and in general pursue what they deem to be important avenues of investigation. Processes of technical development are furthered in such an environment when the institutions at issue make a long-term commitment to the community they support and the research they hope to receive. In other words, technology development is a somewhat simpler and better-understood process of technical change than technology transfer, because it is rooted so firmly in human rather than material capital.

The specific demands technology makes on its environment for support and the possibilities it offers for social and institutional change very much depend on the particularities of individual technologies. Tractors are a capital-intensive technology whose utilization is very dependent upon large-scale holdings and extensive infrastructural support. As such, they present the state with different problems of adoption and often very different capabilities for social and political change than do improved varieties of maize, which are suited to both small- and large-scale farms and whose utilization is not as dependent upon infrastructural support. Similarly, in the case of technology development, the fact that there is a strong technical consensus on which technologies are important and how they should be developed in the area of seeds presents international institutions with a very different technical basis for political development than does the lack of such a consensus in mechanization. Technology itself carries certain requirements of successful development and adoption which are independent determinants of technology's success. These same characteristics offer both the state and international institutions special capabilities to pursue the institutional goals they set for themselves. It is that subject to which I now turn.

Political Institutions and Their Constituencies

The African state pursues programs of agricultural technology development and transfer in order to develop the productive capabilities of its economy and to create the conditions necessary for the establishment of greater national welfare. Technology has also been a terribly important development resource for international assistance agencies. As facilitators of Third World economic development, international aid organizations have occasionally developed new technologies themselves, which have furthered processes of technical change and economic modernization. More frequently, they have mastered an understanding of a particular technical field in order to successfully introduce a technology that is already in the marketplace but is unfamiliar to Third World countries. However, both actors have used these programs as well to maintain and support their own institutional survival. This has entailed the expansion of institutional capabilities and their integration with important constituencies. There is no necessary conflict between these political processes and technical innovation, but some modes of institutional survival are better than others at respecting technology's need for support.

State building is a process of historical change that has been just as dramatically revolutionary as that of technological modernization.[12] In the early sixties the African state was just beginning its state-building journey. Michael Lofchie, looking back on the first decade of African political development, discovered that as the state began its trip down what would inevitably be a very long and rough road, it was attempting to telescope into a few brief years stages of institutional development that took Western states decades or centuries to traverse.[13] With a largely unintegrated society, a weak unindustrial economy, and new, unarticulated institutions, the postindependence state had taken on the task of representing the interests of society as a whole, developing the economy, and creating the foundations of a welfare state. In the West as processes of industrialization were initiated, those classes that suffered the most did not vote; commitments to social equity followed industrialization; and governments that took on the job of social welfare were already able to successfully collect taxes and provide for internal security. In other words, the African state in the 1960s was attempting simultaneously to carry out a number of activities that had been undertaken sequentially in the industrialized world.

Given the number of military coups in Africa in the sixties and the quiet transformations of multiple-party states to single-party systems (frequently personalist governments), it is obvious that Lofchie was right. Something had been out of step between the tasks the state had assumed and the capabilities at its disposal. But what kind of state was this that had begun with democratic forms and retreated to authoritarianism? Some scholars convincingly argued that it was European absolutism that was the most relevant historical model to which the current African state might be compared.[14] Governments in Africa are, according to these analysts, in form if not philosophy, a replication of the authoritarian, bureaucratic, personalist states of a Europe of many centuries ago. This mode of state building is not, according to these theorists, entirely within the choice of modern African societies. They were faced at independence with a certain set of social, economic, and political circumstances. These African states are, like their European counterparts, based on agrarian economies, and are highly heterogeneous, unintegrated social orders, with an institutional legacy of bureaucratic rule. Thus it is hardly surprising that the primary goal of the African state became imposing its institutional presence upon the society and territory for which it has been made responsible.

But while most African states have reshaped their representative institutions to suit the necessity of establishing political control over the social order—in other words, very few are genuinely democratic and most are explicitly and primarily concerned with expanding state power—not all have rid themselves of the social welfare ethic. Fewer still have given up on the notion of using the state to develop the economy. The absolutist state did not engage in prompting or managing economic production to the same extent as do modern governments, and it certainly did not see the economic fruits of its labors as having anything to do with responsibility for the overall welfare of society. In fact, many African states are political hybrids which combine an organizational interest in bureaucratic expansion and social control with an economic agenda and, in some cases, an ethic of social responsibility which is more akin to the modern welfare state. These states speak the political and economic language of the late twentieth century, but they sit astride societies that are peasant, economies that are unindustrialized, and political institutions that are bureaucratic. And, as a consequence, the state building that they sponsor is a blend of old and—for us—unfamiliar goals and methods that are very similar to those of the early modern state in Europe, and goals and methods that are new and more familiar to contemporary Western industrial societies.

State building in Africa entails three interrelated political tasks. The development of an institutional capability to govern—the centralization of power in the hands of the state—is perhaps the primary goal of the contemporary African state. African states inherited a bureaucratic structure from colonial regimes and brought with them a party organization, which had been built to win independence. In both cases these were very insubstantial institutions. Colonial rule had established a strong political tradition of bureaucratic governance, but in terms of sheer material and institutional capability the new state inherited a relatively weak structure. The party or parties that worked for self-government similarly were entirely without contact with many parts of the country they had represented and were overtaxed in respect to both human and material resources. At the time of independence the problem of institutional capability was not fully recognized by either African statesmen or analysts. The euphoria of the postindependence period made it difficult to see that the new political house was built on institutional sand. Immediately following the establishment of new governments, competition among political parties, the bureaucracy, the military, factions within each, and other institutional representatives of the new state erupted into conflicts which in many cases challenged the legitimacy of the new political order. These conflicts were concerned as much with control over very scarce institutional resources as they were with philosophies of rule. The resolution of such conflicts frequently resulted in the further centralization of power in the office of the executive. The new leadership consolidated its hold on the state at the same time that it went in search of the institutional resources to extend its power into the society.

The second goal of African state building is the establishment of a stable constituency upon which to base the founding of political power. After independence there were large portions of society that operated wholly outside of the confines of the new state and its policies. These groups remained more closely tied to village than to national politics. There were also smaller portions of society, the scale of which varied from state to state, which were highly mobilized but which were in conflict with each other and were very frequently the source of the political battles in which the state was immersed. Complicating this distinction between those groups that were mobilized and those that were not were forms of social identity based upon class and ethnicity. Thus, the state confronted a highly heterogeneous social order with more cleavages than sources of common identity. The fragility of the political order was only in part a consequence of weak institutions. In the midst of it all, the state was in search of a permanent coalition of class, ethnic, rural, urban, traditional, and nontraditional groups by which it might govern. The state needed a social base that would survive political setbacks, economic crises, institutional reorganizations, and sustained social and political conflict.

The creation of a rural social relations of production that would buttress the goals of the extension of administrative power and the securing of a stable constituency is the third and final goal of African state building. The state confronted at independence a pattern of rural tenure relations and production control established during the colonial period. This included settler landholdings, European plantations, agricultural enterprises owned by both a European and an African bourgeoisie, African cash crop farmers with land tenure and those without, and a mass of subsistence producers who held their land in common under tribal law. In most cases, the wealthiest members of these groups who were African were tightly linked to the movement for national independence and the new state. Despite this, the state did not always endorse the relations of property that it had inherited but made an autonomous decision to support or redefine them. The establishment of postindependence social relations of agricultural production was rooted in this determination and in the relative availability of public resources to support the productive capabilities of those in control of the land.

If investments in modern technology are to be the mode of transport to carry village economies across a desert of economic underdevelopment to the land of productivity and affluence, the agents who book the journey, sell the tickets, plot the course, and keep the vehicle in good repair may have plans for the new settlement that go beyond depositing passengers at the end of the trip. This relationship of politics to economics is not entirely particular to Africa. But what is unique is the way in which the pursuit of economic development has overlapped with the necessity of building the most basic foundations of early state power. Many societies have confronted problems of economic scarcity and institutional underdevelopment. But in other parts of the world, either the level of economic development was somewhat greater at the point at which central institutions began to expand, or its importance had not yet been established as the state began to extend its authority: it could be compared, relatively speaking, to a wealthy booking agent who could survive the failure of the first few trips, or to an agent who did not have to think twice about indenturing many of the travelers from the very beginning. The attempt to succeed at economic development and use it at the same time as a vehicle for moving through the initial stages of state building is the defining feature of modern African politics.

States differ among themselves in the way they attack the problem of advancing state power and the economy simultaneously. The need to secure the political foundations of state power is common to all, but what differs is the extensiveness of institutional development chosen, the size of the constituency addressed, and the radicalness of the changes to be effected in social relations of production. The two states that we will examine in the coming chapters—Tanzania and Kenya—embrace very similar economic and social circumstances and the same basic state-building goals. But they have defined their own unique directions in respect to the problem of state building. Tanzania has defined broad political participation and a commitment to basic social welfare as essential to its political raison d'être. Kenya, in contrast, has only gradually expanded the political and economic resources of the state to society as a whole. This distinction in constituency choice was rooted in the political philosophies of their respective leaderships and has made all the difference in respect to the way state power has been expanded and the social relations of production defined. It has also been the most important determinant of technological success and failure. It is not state building per se that determines whether technology transfer will succeed or fail, but the ways in which the social foundations of support are defined.

International organizations are similarly involved in a political game that integrates economic with institutional goals. International institutions have been a part of the modern international system for over a century, but formal development assistance programs were only established in the late forties and early fifties, as afterthoughts or alternatives to other, more ambitious world order efforts. The United Nations charter included no commitment to development assistance programs, and the World Bank had been established to assist in the reconstruction of Europe. The Third World was relatively unimportant in the immediate postwar world, but all of that would change rather dramatically as Europe's empire slowly unraveled, and Third World movements for national self-determination claimed their right to state sovereignty. By the 1960s dozens of new states had been created and 45 percent of the membership of the United Nations was composed of these recently independent countries. The impact on international institutions was widespread and long lasting. As Robert Asher would explain, "no previously established international agency can afford to admit that it is not primarily a development agency."[5]

Initially, international aid programs were thought to be logical extensions of other forms of global technical and economic cooperation. On the one hand, they would facilitate the introduction of the same technical norms and standards that were the focus of cooperation among industrial states. On the other hand, they would further the development of a genuine international market, as the Bretton Woods agreements on trade and money had done. From the beginning, however, international aid programs did not act like simple extensions of such efforts. Assistance programs were given a mandate to carry out an operational task, or service, which would result in the development of Third World countries. Development projects, which were the centerpieces of assistance programs, were designed to facilitate direct resource transfers from industrialized to nonindustrialized countries. These projects included policy advice and evaluation missions, which researched development problems and formulated policy; capital assistance, which secured finance and provided loans; technical assistance, which seconded to internal institutions general policy experts and technical personnel; and education and training. International institutions that in many cases had originally been made responsible for furthering agreements on subjects of world order now acted like, and indeed substituted for, domestic institutions that managed, regulated, or promoted the growth of the national economy.

The consequence of the unique requirements of international aid has been the creation of the most highly institutionalized mode of international economic or technical cooperation currently in place. Its critics call it "a cumbersome and overlapping alphabet soup which substitutes bureaucracy for real projects."[16] Even its sympathizers worry about the ways in which a large-scale international bureaucracy is able to relate to the particular technical needs and special economic circumstances of the Third World countries in which it operates.[17] Their primary concern is the fragmentation that exists among the variety of agencies operating in the assistance community and the lack of any clear focus or orientation for the structure of aid as a whole. In other words, they are alarmed by the fact that each international aid agency operates completely independently of other agencies. The politics of international aid is, thus, a politics of organization building. Agencies work hard to create their own fiefdoms within the structure of international aid as a whole. They do so through the search for the institutional capabilities, constituency, and world order goals that will secure a strong position vis à vis other organizations.

Thus, to begin with, international agencies are in pursuit of capabilities that are unique and distinctive and that allow them to centralize power within the agency itself. Each agency adopts a development ideology which defines the perimeters of its program development, budgetary allocations, and assistance projects. The ideology makes clear the special contributions that the agency makes to Third World development. The institutional growth that is fostered as a consequence includes departments and divisions that attend to the particular problem addressed by the agency. This structure is extended in the form of regional and country offices, interagency committees and consortia, and formal agreements to cooperate with a variety of public and private actors engaged in assistance. This is done to communicate and publicize the capabilities of the organization. The agency is primarily interested in establishing its own ability to master development problems, rather than coordinating with other agencies or states.

The creation of a constituency of support is the second task to which international assistance agencies address themselves. Like the state the international agency is in search of a social foundation for the development of its institutional power. The institutional ideology, programmatic development, and budgetary allocations must be constructed in such a way that they meet the perspectives of the agency's constituency. The problem of constituency creation for individual agencies has included the effort to resolve the interests of developed and developing countries; the marshaling of interest among other agencies, friendly and unfriendly; and the mobilization of technical expertise within and without the agency. This mix of external support groups in the form of states and other agencies and internal support groups composed of the technical experts and general policymakers grows out of a highly fragmented institutional environment in which there is great controversy concerning how programs of economic development should be conceptualized and implemented. The need to assess and reassess organizational direction, to accomodate great diversity, and in some instances to carry on assistance activities in the face of serious cleavages in support defines the relationship of the organization to the social foundations of its institutional power.

Finally, the politics of international aid agencies includes the effort on the part of aid agencies to make an impact upon world order. International assistance organizations do not very frequently, if at all, sponsor international negotiations, the writing of international law, or the establishment of international agreements. Nevertheless, they see themselves as agents of such harmonization of international technical and economic policy through the projects they sponsor. Each assistance project is thought to be an embodiment of the technical norms and economic principles championed by the agency in its world order programs and is thus assumed to represent in the Third World those same norms and principles. As the agency's projects themselves succeed in developing Third World countries, they will as well succeed in integrating an approach to national development that will complement and perhaps induce greater interest in international cooperation and world order. It is not simply development per se that the agency wishes to see accomplished but the kind of development that integrates Third World states into international technical and economic agreements of a more far-reaching character.

Thus, international assistance agencies transfer technology to Third World countries within an institutional context not so dissimilar from that of states. Both states and agencies are attempting to find constituencies to support institutional growth and the transformation of broader social and economic relations. Like states, organizations have made very different choices in respect to the scale of the constituencies they address, the extensiveness of institutional development, and the ambitiousness of other economic and social change. In the area of agricultural mechanization, international agencies have chosen to define an approach to assistance that is highly universalistic in nature. Their ambitions in respect to the constituency they serve and the world order goals they hope to accomplish are extensive. In contrast, in the area of seed development, agencies have chosen to sharply limit the consituency they serve and the world order goals they meet. These choices have determined where and when international agencies have been able to effectively cooperate among themselves and where and when they have been able to effectively develop and transfer agricultural technology to Third World countries. As in the case of the state, it is not attention to political development per se that undermines or facilitates the success of technology projects, but the ways in which particular types of political development interact with technical characteristics.

The interaction of technical and political imperatives is in no way a uniform or simple process. This is very much the case in Africa where so many different actors have been involved in efforts to develop the economy. In the coming chapters I will try to delineate which facets of technical and political systems are responsible for significant economic, technical, and political change. There is a very important complementarity between the two and a very difficult contradiction, which helps to explain why some institutions have been more successful than others and why some technologies have had greater impact. I will begin my exploration by examing an area of international aid in which the contradictions seem most pronounced and the constituency for successful technology development and diffusion most elusive.

CHAPTER **2**

AGRICULTURAL MECHANIZATION AND INTERNATIONAL INSTITUTIONAL FRAGMENTATION

THIRD WORLD states come to the problem of agricultural development with great differences in their ecological and economic contexts. In fact, the diversity of Third World farming systems rivals the ethnic and cultural diversity of Third World societies. The international assistance community addresses this diversity of circumstances in the area of agricultural mechanization with technical resources spanning the entire spectrum of technology choice. The goals of the United Nations system and the voluntary agencies that assist it are ambitious. As a consequence, a wide array of projects have been launched—from small-scale efforts for the redesign of peasant technology to large-scale tractorization with projects concerned with animal draft wedged in-between. International assistance agencies have created a veritable technological marketplace in agricultural mechanization.

However, there is no visible or invisible hand in this marketplace guiding agencies to make the most rational technical choices with regard to individual Third World countries. The mechanization projects that are developed speak more frequently to the international institutional imperatives that give them voice than to the unspoken technical requirements of the countries with whom an assistance dialogue is begun. Further, each agency operates in a highly autonomous fashion, vying with others for support within the development assistance community.

The development of multiple and competitive forms of technical assistance in the area of agricultural mechanization is the consequence of the highly universalistic world order goals and broad constituency interests of each agency. The Food and Agriculture Organization (FAO), the International Labor Organization (ILO), and the World Bank each address issues of global economic and technical change of interest to the world community as a whole and in the process attempt to meet the development needs of all Third World countries. While in theory specializing in a particular area of development policy, which would limit their organizational agenda in some respects, in practice they are all involved in very similar development programs and projects. In the case of mechanization, their programs and projects are potentially highly complementary, but the individual institutional commitments of each agency prevent any recognition of the need for cooperation.

It is also the case that while there is no organizational center, no focused constituency, and no common institutional mandate, there is also no powerful normative or technical consensus in the area of agricultural mechanization which might guide the work of this very fragmented institutional structure. Thus, the knowledge at the disposal of international assistance agencies in the area of agricultural mechanization, the advice they might offer, and the projects they can fund are scattered across a number of different institutions for reasons of technical as well as political authority.

The lack of such political authority or technical consensus among assistance agencies on questions of agricultural mechanization would pose few problems for states possessing independent technical capabilities and judgment. But Third World countries, perhaps especially African states, look to international assistance agencies to offer the technical advice and direction they lack. The ideological war over appropriate and inappropriate technology, the competitive institutional capabilities, and the strong commitments of each agency to its own founding mandate make it difficult for countries seeking assistance to receive advice that is tailored to their own special needs.

In this chapter I examine how technology projects have been developed in this context of competitive and fragmented international assistance.

The Food and Agriculture Organization

The FAO was created to conquer the problem of world hunger. The long bread lines of the thirties, the starvation associated with the war, and the number of displaced refugees in the late forties and the hardships they faced were the common experiences that prompted an interest in the creation of an international agency whose sole concern was food. As importantly, at the time that the FAO was created, the knowledge and technical understanding available seemed to offer the practical possibility that other countries and future generations need not suffer the scourge of famine or malnutrition. To quote from one of the earlier FAO statements on its own mandate:

> The Food and Agriculture Organization is born out of the idea of freedom from want. This is not one man's fortunate phrase; it expresses an aspiration as old as mankind. When primitive men tried to imagine paradise in concrete terms, they pictured it as a place where food was plentiful and want no longer existed. Every utopia man has conceived has been such a place. But in this generation freedom from want has come to have a different meaning. It has been taken out of the realm of utopian ideas. The conviction has spread that it can be achieved; indeed, this is one of the convictions most characteristic of the thinking of and the mood of this generation.[1]

Productivity could be dramatically increased, food crises avoided, and international supplies secured because man now had at his disposal the technical capability to develop agriculture and provide for food emergencies. The FAO celebrated the sophistication of modern agricultural technology and linked it directly to its pursuit of a world in which no one faced starvation.

The FAO was asked to address the problem of hunger and food in two respects. It was given responsibility for international trade in agricultural products and the development of stronger agricultural sectors. While the FAO's role in assessing the international availability of food continues to be utilized in times of international disaster, states rather vigorously battled for the right to control their agricultural trade. Development assistance, as a result, became the primary international task of the organization. The creation of greater production capability superceded the need to regulate or distribute international stocks, but it did not redefine the agency's commitment to broad-scale global interests.[2]

In 1950, the FAO was given a budget of $5 million and a staff of 507 professionals.[3] It had inherited some field projects from other UN agencies, but in the main its work was done in its own offices, not in the field. In 1956 the FAO was supporting 500 field experts in fifty-eight countries; by 1966 it had 1,683 professionals in the field.[4] In 1966 the total budget for the organization was just over $167 million; in 1976, it was $606 million.[5] In both cases, development assistance programs and projects were supported by three-quarters of total agency funds. Thus, in less than a decade, the promotion of agricultural development overtook the promotion of interstate cooperation; in just over a decade, development assistance dominated the activities of the agency. Solving the problem of world hunger became almost entirely linked to the development of Third World agriculture.

The organizational structure of the FAO is like that of many other international agencies. Functional divisions define the basic institutional skeleton of the organization. There are programs defined by types of technologies, crops, economic policies, social issues, and agricultural services. In the 1960s as it assumed more responsibility for in-field projects, the organization began to make efforts to decentralize and send more permanent staff into the field. In 1974 country desks were created and later the country post of senior agricultural advisor. The addition of nationally and regionally oriented departments gave the organization a greater potential capability to respond to national needs and contexts, but it did not result in any changes of authority. The policy direction for the agency's work was set in Rome.

The ideology that guides the FAO's program of assistance stressed the importance of a vigorous private sector and the transfer of modern technology and expertise. Both were thought to establish a basis for high levels of productivity, and thus overall growth in the agricultural sector. The criteria for program or project success were quite clear. If the free market were allowed to operate, if capital-intensive, technically sophisticated technology were transferred, and/or if the agricultural economy got high yields per acre and high rates of growth, the organization considered itself successful. When the winds of ideological change swept through the development assistance community in the late sixties, the FAO was almost impervious to the arguments made by internal and external exponents of a basic needs or rural income approach. An early study within the FAO calling for an FAO commitment to rural welfare which would meet "the most basic needs of food, housing, and clothing"[6] never really made an impact on the goals or programs of the agency as a whole.

The projects in agricultural mechanization that have been sponsored by the FAO are legion. While beginning with a modest effort, the organization rapidly expanded its capabilities in this area. In 1956–57 the FAO's Agricultural Engineering Service sponsored fourteen field projects and four advice missions; in 1964–65 it supported 122 field experts; in 1976–77 it was responsible for two-hundred projects.[7] Like all UN specialized agencies, the FAO's aid is primarily in the area of technical assistance, but its work in this area has embraced agricultural mechanization projects which include farm construction, the mechanization of agricultural processing, the support of rural industry, and the mechanization of basic production.[8] In theory the FAO has been interested in all levels of mechanization, including research into small-scale technologies and improvements in animal draft. And indeed, in the earliest years of FAO assistance, there were projects that addressed such problems.[9] But the modal FAO agricultural mechanization project is concerned with the introduction of the tractor.

According to the FAO, tractors are an extremely important technological resource for Third World countries in the throes of developing their agricultural sectors; because if allowed to work to their fullest technical potential, tractors produce more. The FAO has held to this view despite the difficulties posed to the introduction of the technology. Beginning in the early fifties, the Agricultural Engineering Service became involved in the support of missions and field projects which provided the planning, expertise, repair, maintenance, and training needed for the introduction of tractors. It became aware at the same time that tractors were not easily integrated into Third World agriculture. To quote from a 1954 assessment:

The story about tractors newly brought into the district unaccustomed to them is the same almost everywhere. Briefly, it is one of frequent breakdown, poor repair, and short lived machines. . . . Graveyards of rusting, unserviceable, and at times, unrepairable machinery have resulted, and these, in some countries where public money was involved, have led to political troubles.[10]

Problems posed by small-scale production systems, the lack of infrastructure, and the unavailability of sufficient capital found in many Third World agricultural sectors led the FAO in several directions, all of which reaffirmed the importance of tractors. It sponsored projects that would clean up technological disasters when the technology was not fully supported. It defined peasant mechanization projects so as to be able to introduce the tractor into circumstances that were not especially conducive to its survival. In the 1960s the FAO created tractor hire services (THSs) in new African nations where one-acre holdings were the norm. These cooperative tractor services allowed small-scale farmers who could not afford to own a tractor to rent one. In the 1970s the FAO proposed the development of projects in which large-scale holdings would be mechanized, and then, once mechanization had been fully established, disaggregated.[11] The FAO has become increasingly sophisticated in its ability to plan for and design projects that will provide support for Third World countries that are interested in the tractor but without the necessary requisites of technology adoption. As in the case of other aid agencies, it was in pursuit of a technical formula that would work for the Third World as a whole.

A challenge to the approach of the Agricultural Engineering Service was articulated by the FAO Policy Analysis Division in the 1970s. K. D. Abercrombie, the deputy director of the division, explains:

> The technology that will increase production fastest is not necessarily that which will increase employment fastest. In this respect mechanization is a particularly crucial component of agricultural technology. There are obviously many circumstances where it is essential for achieving the required increase in production. But, unless it is used wisely, it can lead to the undesirable displacement of labor.[12]

Abercrombie is concerned with issues of rural welfare. He calls for more research on the national level, for a mechanization program for small farmers, and for a more careful consideration of the assumptions underlying a uniform technology policy. Less concerned with the problem of technical failure, more interested in the economic impact of the introduction of a capital-intensive technology on Third World agricultural sectors, Abercrombie attempts to set a new direction for the agency.

The FAO is now sponsoring some small-scale mechanization projects, but in the main continues to support a program of tractorization. The ideology of the organization, which emphasizes the importance of large-scale production increases and identifies capital-intensive technology as the route to increased production, supports only one technology choice. The institutional structure and capabilities are similarly biased in support of large-scale mechanization. There are other assistance agencies that take the technical failures experienced by the FAO and the admonitions of Abercrombie seriously, but the FAO as a whole is quite confident of the value of the technology it advocates.

The Intermediate Technology Development Group

The Intermediate Technology Development Group (ITDG) is an assistance organization of a distinctively different character than the FAO. It pursues a very narrow technical agenda, sponsors research as well as diffusion projects, and is as interested in a constituency of technical experts as with the states in which it operates. It is a voluntary assistance agency that was established by E. F. Schumacher, George McRobie, and several other fellow travelers in 1965 to promote the idea of intermediate technology. Convinced that Third World countries were adopting technologies that were well suited to the country of origin but not the country of adoption, Schumacher and friends planned to offer technological advice and resources that Third World countries would find more appropriate to the constraints they faced and more conducive to the promotion of economic welfare, not growth. They also hoped to revolutionize the assistance community and redirect the programs of well-established agencies:

> I think it is very easy to fall into the trap that the official aid agencies have deliberately fallen into and this is to say, "We cannot be anything until we have received requests from developing countries." The first task is to make known that there are alternatives and then a demand might be forthcoming.[13]

TABLE 2.1.   ITDG Income and Expenditure, 1970–1975 (in pounds)

	1970	1971	1972	1973	1974	1975
			Central Organization			
Income	22,074	22,950	56,812	69,139	82,354	97,683
Expenditure	25,734	26,365	45,006	71,658	85,900	88,296
			Projects			
Income	47,614	52,532	66,654	71,429	73,776	219,957
Expenditure	26,983	53,086	61,480	69,803	79,194	158,407

SOURCE: ITDG, *Annual Reports, 1970–75* (London).

The ITDG, despite the ambitious political task it set for itself, remained a small organization. In 1975 it spent £158,407 on projects and £88,296 on central-office expenditures (see table 2.1). This is a tiny fraction of what the average UN assistance organization is able to allocate to either. In terms of staff, the ITDG ran its operations in 1970 with an office crew of five professionals. This gradually increased, although by 1975 the organization was only supported in London by twelve professionals, many of whom were concerned with publications and accounts. The group is a registered charity and nonprofit company which presently owns three subsidiaries—Inter-Technology Services Ltd., Development Techniques Ltd., and Intermediate Publications Ltd. Neither the income earned from the activities of these companies nor the donations of private individuals and foundations resulted in the kind of budget that would support a large program of projects.

The organizational structure of the ITDG made a virtue of necessity, but it also integrated itself into the British technical community. In an effort to get beyond the limitations of its own financial resources, a network of consultants was established. Panels covering the areas in which projects were sponsored—agriculture, construction, cooperatives, chemistry, forestry, ferro-cement, power, rural health, transportation, and water—were composed of experts associated with British universities, government, industry, research institutes, and other economic and technological institutions. The network is based upon the same principle of organizational development as is the FAO—functional policy areas. The panels draw upon a wide range of experience and expertise, assist in the answering of technical inquiries, aid in the preparation of publications, and guide in the execution of projects. However, the primary distinction between the ITDG's approach and that of other aid agencies is that the agency draws upon the resources and catalyzes the activities of other institutions instead of creating its own in-house capability.

The ideology that set the foundation of the ITDG's efforts grew from the work of one its founders, E. F. Schumacher. It was his exposure to Gandhi's philosophy of village development—small-scale manufacture and the handicraft industry—that led Schumacher to coin the term "intermediate technology."[14] Intermediate technology was technology that would draw upon indigenous resources in the fullest respect and construct a foundation for development that was strongly rooted in the traditional sector. Intermediate technology was technology that was labor intensive, suited to the level of education of the society as a whole, and produced of local materials.[15] For Schumacher, development was inevitably an evolutionary process of change, requiring incremental progress in the education, organization, and discipline of individual societies. The introduction of highly sophisticated and capital-intensive technologies, without the appropriate supports, resulted in development that was restricted to the social and economic environments possessing the necessary modern infrastructure. The rest of society, and the larger economic potential of the country, remains on the periphery of development. The introduction of intermediate technology would, on the other hand, integrate the larger economic and social environment into the process of modernization and base developmental change on the capabilities and needs of the entire society. For Schumacher, technology was either one component of a process of historical change in which a nation's peoples fully participate, or an agent for skipping important development stages, and the majority of the population along with them. To quote from Schumacher:

> One cannot "jump" in development, because education does not jump; education is a gradual process. Organization does not jump; it must evolve to fit changing circumstances and the same goes for discipline. All three cannot be ordered or simply planned; they must evolve step by step and the foremost task of policy must be to speed this evolution.[16]

The ITDG's efforts to revolutionize assistance in the area of mechanical technology has been most constrained by the fact that its assistance accomplishments have been modest.[17] It has sponsored a variety of research in technical innovation and has collected the results of research done by others. The ITDG publishes aspects of this research, which includes complete sets of technical drawings for various kinds of small-scale equipment. It has also made visible available technology long on the market but not well known. One of its earliest and most frequently revised publications, *Tools for Progress*, a guide to simple tools, is a collection of technology that the ITDG believes is especially appropriate to the economic circumstances of Third World countries, but that is manufactured and sold by small companies with low visibility. Other bibliographies and guides to technology have followed, among which is a work specifically devoted to agricultural technology. The group has also carried out technology transfer projects. Policy advice and evaluation missions have been carried out in twenty-four countries, half of those in Africa. In the case of agriculture, three have concerned the question of ox-drawn equipment and agricultural mechanization. Such missions have had various results—the establishment of national technology programs, the creation of appropriate technology units within government ministries or at universities, and the implementation of assistance projects. Technical-assistance field projects have been carried out in nearly every sector for which there is an ITDG panel. In agriculture, the ITDG's most ambitious projects have centered on agricultural mechanization in Nigeria and Zambia. Both projects were carried out between 1971 and 1974, and concerned the introduction of animal-drawn equipment. The ITDG emphasized the importance of farm surveys and research in order to define the characteristics of the farming systems prior to the identification or design of appropriate technology.

Many administrators within the development assistance community ridicule the projects of the ITDG for their quirky technical foci and their small-scale approach. Who cares if one village in one African country is experimenting with windmills? Like Don Quixote, say UN experts, Schumacher's team of technical innovators are only tilting at the problem of development. At the same time, each of the UN agencies under review here profited from an early association with the ITDG and/or careful consideration of the work of Schumacher. None were, however, interested in acknowledging to the ITDG the role of leadership that it sought for itself. This might not have been the case had the ITDG been able to manufacture the kind of technological breakthrough in mechanization that riveted the international assistance community in the area of seed technology.

International Labor Organization

The ILO was founded after World War I. An institutional child of the social transformations that embraced Europe and the United States in the early twentieth century, the ILO internationalized the proletarian ideal of change in the workplace. The early programs of the ILO were concerned with freedom of association, nondiscrimination, the obligations of management to labor, the security of employment, and the like. The organization undertook the research necessary for, and drafted and monitored, international law in the area of labor relations and the safety of factory conditions.[18]

Dissatisfaction with the ILO's approach to social justice and world order was expressed by the earliest Third World members. How could questions of workers' rights be properly addressed in countries where the foundations of modern economic production were not yet developed? Latin American and Asian member states introduced this concern in the fifties and pushed for an agency with a commitment to economic change. In 1950 80 percent of the ILO's budget was spent on social legislation, in 1958 it was 44 percent, and by 1967 only 16 percent of the funds allocated to the ILO from member states and the United Nations was spent on its traditional work program.[19] The organization instituted programs in vocational training, manpower planning, cooperatives, small-scale industry, and rural handicrafts. Each of these areas expressed the ILO's interest in workers, but productivity and GNP growth began to replace the drafting of normative agreements as indicators of organizational success. The ILO by the early sixties had become a full-fledged development assistance agency.[20]

The ILO was never entirely comfortable with the marriage of these two concerns. In its attempt to meet the needs of two separate constituencies—developed and developing countries—it embraced two ideologies, two sets of programs, and institutional capabilities to match each. In 1969

TABLE 2.2. ILO Technical Assistance Expenditures in All Countries, 1950–1969

	Equipment	
Category	$ U.S.	% of Total Cost
Human resources development:	15,791,351	88.0
Manpower planning and organization	332,091	1.9
Management development	3,721,134	20.7
Small industries and handicrafts	1,180,293	6.6
Vocational training	10,557,833	58.8
Conditions of work and life:	1,061,863	5.9
Social security	14,154	0.1
Occupational safety and health	1,012,758	5.6
General conditions of work	34,951	0.2
Social institutions development:	1,086,655	6.1
Labor law and labor relations	18,136	0.1
Labor administration	68,858	0.4
Workers' education	44,771	0.3
Cooperative, rural, and related institutions development	954,890	100.0
TOTAL	17,939,869	

SOURCE: Thomas George Weiss, *International Bureaucracy* (Toronto: Heath, 1975), p. 126.

David Morse, the director general of the ILO, proposed a new assistance direction for the agency. To more successfully integrate the ILO's commitment to social welfare with its interest in economic change in the Third World, Morse introduced the World Employment Program (WEP). The WEP would include the traditional concerns of the ILO with labor, full employment, and social progress and at the same time address the conditions of underemployment and unemployment found in the Third World.[21]

The organizational structure of the ILO is very similar to that of the FAO. It is functional in nature with a host of divisions and departments defined in respect to particular areas of social and economic policy. The World Employment Program, for example, includes branches working on income distribution, population, education, urbanization, rural poverty, emergency employment schemes, international migration, multinational corporations, the international division of labor, and technology. The

ILO has made almost no attempt to decentralize its operations and did not adopt the FAO plan for country desks or country representatives.

The ideology that has guided the work of the agency has varied. The ILO once ascribed to a theory of economic development and change very similar to that of the FAO. The need to introduce modern methods and techniques and to make economic productivity the primary assistance goal, as well as the fostering of conditions in which private investment might thrive, were at the center of the ILO's effort. This did not result in the launching of large-scale technology projects, but it did result in the transfer of standards in the areas of education, social security legislation, occupational health and safety, national employment services, and labor administration, which were particularly well suited to modern, industrialized societies. With the launching of the WEP, the ILO directly challenged ideologies of development that stressed economic productivity and/or social modernization. It rejected its own support of this approach and articulated a strategy of basic needs.[22] A basic needs program of development assistance would stress the importance of social and economic equity and set out strategies for the creation of income and services for the average member of Third World societies. The measure of success would not lie in the overall growth of the economy but in indicators of welfare—average income, income distribution, the availability of education, rates of malnutrition, the provision of health services, the accessibility of housing, and life expectancy. The goal of the agency in these areas was, as in the case of the FAO, to trigger global change.

The ILO has not specialized in agricultural mechanization, but it has addressed the problem through some early field projects, in-house research, and country employment missions. Technology was identified by the WEP as a particularly important resource because it possessed the capability to trigger changes in basic development direction. According to Keith Marsden, the architect of the ILO's technology program, labor-intensive, small-scale technology stimulates growth from the bottom up. It creates jobs in the traditional economic sector in which the majority of the population is involved and increases income for a large number of people.[23] Some of the research sponsored by the WEP's Technology Branch is concerned with agricultural mechanization, and one member of the staff has studied the role of tractors in the displacement of labor in

Asia.[24] Many of the WEP's policy advice and evaluation missions, especially those carried out in Africa, addressed the issue. The ILO's reluctance to fund technical assistance or to transfer technology, per se, means that it relies to a even greater degree than the FAO or the ITDG on the willingness of Third World governments to invest resources in projects that it recommends but does not implement.[25] In general, the ILO's mechanization projects were seen as vehicles for changing the overall development strategies of Third World states.

The World Bank

The World Bank was created at the end of World War II as a part of the Bretton Woods negotiations, which also established the International Monetary Fund (IMF) and laid the foundation of the General Agreement on Tariffs and Trade. In the most general sense, it was the Bank's duty, along with the IMF, to see that Third World countries adopted the economic policies to which industrial states committed themselves at Bretton Woods. This meant the development of economies open to international trade and investment, nonprotectionist and fiscally conservative in temperament, ready to take advantage of the resources private corporations might offer. This system of international organization was to assure an international economy free from the crises that wracked the system in the thirties and helped, according to many commentators, to cause World War II. Very quickly, the Bank became the most credible judge of the economic capabilities and future of Third World states. Bank decisions on assistance were taken as indicators of the potential of an economy and the policy climate of the state.

The resources at the disposal of the World Bank are considerable. By 1974 the Bank had lent $30.4 billion to Third World countries; by 1978 the total had grown to $58.4 billion.[26] For many Third World countries the Bank is the single largest supplier of capital assistance. In the early sixties, a very small percentage of Bank loans went to agriculture. In fact, between 1961 and 1971 the Bank allocated 31.9 percent of its funds to transportation and 31.8 percent to power. This began to change in the latter half of the decade. Between 1963 and 1968 the Bank invested $600 million in agricultural development—almost as much in five years as it had invested in the preceding sixteen. By 1970 total capital outlays in agriculture had increased to 13.1 percent of total World Bank lending.[27] In 1978, in terms of cumulative lending, agriculture was the largest sector, having overtaken both power and transportation.[28]

The structure of the World Bank is multifaceted. To begin with, it is composed of two separate lending operations, the International Bank for Reconstruction and Development (IBRD) and the International Development Agency (IDA). Each offer different terms upon which loans can be extended; both are governed and administered within the same framework. The Bank has functional divisions defined by the sectors of the economy to which it most consistently lends its funds—transportation, power, education, agriculture, and the like. It also includes in-house regional departments which are directly responsible for projects and which in some instances include staff with technical, not economic, expertise. The power is relatively equally divided between these two administrative units. Further, the Bank has regional field offices and in some cases country representatives who monitor projects and participate in planning. Unlike other international assistance agencies, the Bank's interest in national policy evaluation and follow-up is relatively well developed. There is a conscious attempt on the part of the institution to relate functional goals to national requirements.

The World Bank began its lending operations with an ideology of development that identified the private investor as the most important catalyst of development.[29] Multinational corporations or private investors internal to Third World countries were seen as the real movers and shakers of economic change. They possessed the skills and the resources necessary to produce economic takeoff. Public institutions such as the World Bank or Third World governments were thought to play a secondary role to the private investor. Their energies were best utilized in the creation of public infrastructures such as power and transport. Bank loans were not to support directly productive activities. The most powerful indicators of economic success were taken to be growth in gross national product, the establishment of an industrial sector, and the overall productivity of agricultural, industrial, and service sectors. A most dramatic change took place in the late sixties when Robert McNamara assumed the presidency. The Bank had been experimenting for several years with loans

TABLE 2.3. World Bank/IDA Lending for Agriculture, by Subsector, FY 1948–1974

	1948–60	1961–65	1966–70	1971–72	1973–74
			$ million		
General agriculture	43.9	—	15.0	13.5	24.0
Agricultural credit	20.2	45.0	183.2	255.8	240.3
Area development	10.0	9.7	100.4	51.6	272.6
Irrigation	85.1	383.8	513.2	201.3	621.9
Livestock	7.0	35.3	252.4	176.7	314.9
Agricultural industries	4.7	—	19.2	39.6	204.0
Non-food crops	—	2.8	86.8	95.4	167.3
Research	—	—	—	12.7	—
Fisheries	—	7.8	21.0	8.9	28.6
Forestry	5.0	—	16.4	—	20.0
TOTAL	175.9	484.4	1,207.6	855.5	1,893.6
			Percentages		
General agriculture	25	—	1	1	1
Agricultural credit	11	9	15	30	13
Area development	6	2	8	6	14
Irrigation	48	79	43	24	33
Livestock	4	7	21	21	17
Agricultural industries	3	—	2	5	11
Non-food crops	—	1	7	11	9
Research	—	—	—	1	—
Fisheries	—	2	2	1	1
Forestry	3	—	1	—	1
TOTAL	100	100	100	100	100

SOURCE: World Bank, *Rural Development-Sector Policy Paper*, Annex 9 (February 1975), p. 85.

in areas like agriculture and education and explained these changes in a relatively pragmatic fashion—Third World countries needed such assistance. But McNamara went much further in his challenge to the institution's raison d'être. He rather quickly assumed an international position as a spokesman for the new ideological perspective which stressed the need to reach the poor through investments in a variety of areas normally thought to be the purview of private actors.[30] His annual addresses became passionate statements of who the poor were, how their incomes in many cases had fallen as a result of two decades of assistance, and what needed to be done to reverse the conditions of Third World poverty.[31] The Bank emerged with an ideology of development that stressed the role of public investment in productive activities, especially agriculture, that measured success in respect to the income of the poorest 40 percent of society, and that took as its primary economic goals equity, not growth.

While the World Bank does not have an agricultural engineering service or a technology division of extensive responsibilities, it has consistently been involved in agricultural mechanization through its lending in agriculture in general. The first Bank loan to a less developed country included credit for the purchase of agricultural machinery. Between 1948 and 1963 $48.5 million was lent in support of agricultural credit for the purchase of tractors and other forms of modern mechanization. Agricultural credit projects were gradually diversified in the sixties, but between 1964 and 1968 agricultural mechanization was second only to livestock in respect to scale of investment.[32] Large-scale mechanization continued to be assisted through other types of projects as well. This was very much in keeping with the kinds of projects the Bank supported in agriculture as a whole. Agriculture projects were on a large scale, dependent upon capital-intensive technology, and important to the country's export sector.

Like the FAO the World Bank was aware that the introduction of tractors posed problems given local economic and technical circumstances. In 1953 the Technical Operations Department wrote:

> In most countries, the use of mechanized equipment is relatively new. Too much cannot be expected from the private dealer's organizations, the farmer's cooperatives, repair shop facilities, and other links in the chain between the manufacturer and ultimate consumer. Therefore, assistance by governmental or semi-governmental organizations, such as a Development Corporation may be warranted.[33]

How to market and maintain tractors was no easy task in countries in which the infrastructure was so sparse. Nevertheless, the World Bank was firmly in support of large-scale, capital-intensive technology. The reasons for this were a function of both the benefits the Bank believed to flow from such technology—growth, productivity—and its institutional capabilities, which were best suited to the design and execution of large-scale projects.[34] On the heels of McNamara's arrival, a direct challenge was posed to large-scale mechanization loans and the previous technical formula. The challenge was, like that at the FAO, raised on the basis of impact, not execution.[35] Like the FAO's Policy Analysis Division and the ILO's Technology Branch of the WEP, some Bank staff were worried about the support of technology that displaced labor and lowered rural income. Three tractorization loans had been approved for India and Pakistan between 1964 and 1968. In the process of reviewing the projects for a second set of loans, the Bank reconsidered its agricultural mechanization policy in light of these new concerns. The loans were successfully renewed, but the war that would break out in the following decade between small- and large-scale technology advocates had been declared.

By the early seventies there were two technology camps in the World Bank. Bank staff concerned with the negative impact of previous technology support began to advocate the introduction of small-scale or appropriate technology. In response to this concern, and building upon McNamara's interest in reaching the poor, the Bank initiated a number of new types of projects including support for ox cultivation rather than tractorization in the area of agricultural technology.[36] These types of projects required more planning and research as well as a change in methods of implementation and supervision. As was the case in the FAO and the ILO, the personnel most comfortable with such changes were located in functional divisions, especially those concerned with economic planning and policy. There were other divisions that remained convinced of the efficacy of earlier projects. Some members of the Bank's staff believed that technical and not economic criteria must, in the first instance, be employed in the design of technology projects. The sophistication and power of the technology to survive difficult physical and economic environments must come first, according to this group. Not entirely coincidentally, this group was also not convinced of the wisdom of McNamara's approach and continued to support the notion that economic growth was as important as overall increases in rural income.

These two technology camps were in conflict with one another throughout the seventies. According to one exponent of the large-scale technology perspective, in regard to agricultural mechanization important issues of immediate relevance to Third World countries had become ideological hot potatoes:

Issues regarding farm mechanization and related aspects of employment are repeatedly raised in the Bank without getting any closer to resolution or agreement. I contend that no amount of general theory or rhetoric will resolve issues; however, I do believe that through deliberate analytical analysis, combined with logic, engineering and economic principles, that we can establish acceptable guidelines regarding agricultural mechanization.[37]

Technology projects became part of the debate that McNamara's change in policy had occasioned. The differences between those who were most sympathetic with the previous ideology and those who were not created a cleavage which split the institution in terms of organizational structure, access to resources, and project design. There were no efforts between the two mechanization camps, for example, to launch an agricultural technology program that included both small- and large-scale technology. As was the case for so many development assistance agencies, each type of technology symbolized a particular set of development goals and was part of an organizational battle primarily concerned with how the organization's global mandate would be defined.

Technology, Constituency, and Institutional Capability

The potential assistance resources at the disposal of Third World states in the area of agricultural mechanization are considerable. The FAO has had wide-ranging experience in the provision of technical assistance, and the World Bank in the provision of capital assistance for the introduction of tractors. The ITDG, the ILO, and the World Bank all have the capability to research, develop, and carry out small-scale mechanization projects. The FAO is associated with important multinational corporations which operate in the technology market; the ITDG has access to British research institutes; and the World Bank is a close partner of many in the international financial community. Added to this are the many mission reports, planning efforts, and sector and technology assessments that address the problem of agricultural mechanization and inform the policymaking of each agency. What more could a country interested in mechanization ask for?

There is really no question that the system as a whole has the necessary resources to meet the needs of Third World countries. What is problematic is the way in which these resources are made available. Each agency is in pursuit of its own private constituency and its own special impact upon world order. This pursuit is firmly rooted in the independent foundings of each institution and results in entirely autonomous institutional development. Despite the creation of the United Nations Development Program (UNDP) in the 1960s, assistance is more closely integrated into the institutional purpose of each agency than it is to the overarching development goals of the system as a whole. Each agency must put a coherent program together, one that links its international commitments to its assistance effort and distinguishes itself from other agencies. The projects it sponsors become the evidence for its distinctive contribution to Third World economic change and concrete proof to its constituency of its need for special budgetary support. Such organizational individualism results in an overall fragmentation of assistance capabilities.

The distinctiveness of each agency's contribution to international cooperation made sense as long as international institutions were primarily concerned with the tasks of promoting international law, standards, and normative agreements. The FAO worked in the area of agricultural trade, the ILO in that of labor regulation, and the World Bank in macroeconomic policy. Their staff and internal expertise were of fundamentally different natures. The ministers and diplomatic staff that composed the national delegations attending annual conferences and budgetary reviews were not the same. These special areas of competence were complemented by the work of a host of other international organizations—UNESCO in education, World Health Organization (WHO) in health, the International Atomic Energy Agency (IAEA) in nuclear energy, as well as others. However, the distinctiveness of these concerns waned as each agency took on more responsibilities for assistance. The attempt to implement an assistance project in the area of agriculture could only be carried out in a limited number of ways. In respect to the staff and the internal capabilities that were needed and in terms of the national constituencies to which each agency made its appeal, the similarities began to outweigh the differences. A rural development project that would increase agricultural productivity, raise rural income, meet the needs of local labor, or assure the financial solvency of the the country as a whole was a rural development project, whether it was carried out by the FAO, the ITDG, the ILO, or the World Bank.

Impatient with the individual world order goals of the UN specialized agencies, the ITDG launched a campaign for greater interagency cooperation in the area of appropriate technology. It attended annual conferences and technical meetings within the UN system to plea for the idea of institutional cooperation and technology research. The FAO has used ITDG consultants; the ILO relied on Schumacher's personal diplomacy to establish ILO projects; the World Bank sent staff members to London in order to incorporate ITDG research into its own programs. The ITDG's work was assimilated into the programs of multilateral assistance agencies, but it did not give birth to interagency cooperation of any consequence. Without a major technology research or diffusion success, the ITDG was unable to garner greater support, and the formation of an international cooperative arrangement in the area of agricultural mechanization or more broadly mechanical technology and engineering was held hostage to the organizational autonomy of each agency and the universalism of the system as a whole. The lack of such an arrangment has made the design and implementation of mechanization projects a less successful endeavor than might otherwise have been the case.

CHAPTER 3

THE MECHANIZATION OF EAST AFRICAN
STATE BUILDING

WITH INDEPENDENCE the new Tanzanian leadership was uncertain about the exact character of its socialism. A debate ensued which was concerned with what kind of social order was most just, and how active an agent of social change the state should be. In other words, what was the most important constituency of the state? How extensively should it develop its institutions to meet the needs of that constituency? And, would such a process of constituency building entail changing the social relations of production? The position that the state adopted on agricultural mechanization reflected the political phases of uncertainty, debate, and commitment which typified the political search for a strategy of state building. The tractor, because of the opportunities for social change that it offered, eventually took on a very special role as a powerful instrument of social revolution.

There was no confusion or uncertainty in Kenya about the social foundations of political power. At independence the people for whom land alienation was most economically and socially devastating, who formed the core of the Mau Mau movement, and who gave Kenya the leader of this nationalist movement, inherited the state. The Kikuyu and their economic and political interests were the guiding spirit of the new postindependence institutions. The problematique of postindependence politics was how to maintain the centrality of the Kikuyu's power, and at the same time find a stable basis for government. Technical resources were occasionally extended to other groups in order to buy legitimacy and maintain order. But the character of that resource investment was limited, and it was always those closest to the state who benefited the most. Thus, the state adopted a strategy of state building that defined its constituency very narrowly and focused its pattern of technology transfer accordingly.

International assistance agencies came and went with any shifts that took place in internal political direction. Agencies emphasized the distinctiveness of their own approaches to the problem of mechanization and defined projects to suit their own broadly defined development goals. They carried out these projects without consultation or resource coordination with other agencies and in general competed for the attention and interest of the state. This meant that there was no policy of long-term planning or follow-up and that individual projects were isolated from one another. International fragmentation resulted in disjointed national programs.

Technical characteristics interacted with political imperatives in surprising ways. This was especially the case for the tractor. In this chapter I will investigate how the extensiveness of the demands that the tractor makes on its environment interact with strategies of state building to produce two very different developmental outcomes; why the tractor was a more attractive political development resource than small-scale technology; and how a fragmented structure of assistance led to the predominance of national over international decision making.

Securing the Social Foundations of State Power

Both Kenya and Tanzania began programs of agricultural mechanization with careful attention given to the social and political impacts of such efforts. In Tanzania there was initial uncertainty about which constituencies were most important, but Julius K. Nyerere like Jomo Kenyatta began to formulate an approach to traditional society that would integrate the social order into the political. Nyerere, Tanzania's first head of state, was an egalitarian, while Kenyatta, Kenya's nationalist leader and first Prime Minister, was an elitist. Into these very different political contexts came the technical resources of international aid agencies. Early assistance was largely concerned with the introduction of the tractor. The importance of this resource did not need to be demonstrated to either country. The British had begun peasant cultivation schemes in Tanzania in the 1950s, and Kenyan settler agriculture was highly mechanized at the time of independence. Further, the constituencies both of these countries hoped to serve, though very different in many respects, were based on large-scale agriculture, and thus highly amenable to large-scale mechanization. However, while in general both countries knew their technological interests, in specific, neither was able to design or carry out its own programs. Tanzania, with very few internal technical capabilities, was especially dependent upon the advice provided by early assistance participants.

In the spring of 1959, and again the following year, a World Bank team of development experts descended upon the soon-to-be-independent Tanzania in order to survey the prospects of its economic development. It was a comprehensive policy and advice mission, but its most in-depth economic review concerned agriculture. The planning framework that was established consisted of two separate approaches to the development of agriculture, titled the "improvement" and the "transformation" approaches.[1] The success of the improvement approach was to be based on the efforts to persuade individual progressive farmers to adopt new methods and techniques. It would concentrate on regions of the country and crops that were already relatively well developed and that would speedily increase marketed production. In contrast, the transformation approach was to include the interjection of outside resources in the form of farm planning, and the creation of infrastructure, management, and capital, and would resettle peasant producers in areas more supportive of successful cultivation. It would address the problem of restructuring the economic and social basis of peasants who were not yet integrated into the market.

Tanzania's own political direction—should peasants be resettled? should they be transformed?—was much more abstract and difficult to connect to the concrete proposals of the World Bank. Nyerere's earliest statements on the political direction of Tanzania reflected his belief that traditional society provided a basis for a new kind of African socialism. He was initially, however, steadfast in his claim that socialism as Africans would practice it "has nothing to do with the possession or nonpossession of wealth," or with the concept of class. It was most fundamentally an "attitude of mind."[2] At the same time, Nyerere used economic as well as social and political referents when he tried to describe the particulars of the traditional social order. His idealization of society was highly communitarian in nature, with the equality of both economic condition and opportunity important features of his model. Nyerere's own intellectual roots were in the Enlightenment and his theory of *ujamaa* (familyhood) in the early sixties anticipated categories of historical materialism in just the same way that Rousseau's theory of the social contract anticipated Marx.

In its report the World Bank warned explicitly that the costs of transformation agriculture and resettlement might be too high, "if mechanization is involved."[3] But the general recommendations associated with the new policy seemed to contradict this rather specific technology choice suggestion. The call for capital-intensive investments and radical changes in methods of cultivation set a context for the introduction of large-scale mechanization.[4] As importantly, Nyerere adopted the Bank's recommendations on transformation agriculture as the technical expression of his communitarian ideal.[5] Ujamaa was thus translated into a village settlement program via the Bank's transformation agriculture with mechanization as the inducement.

There were many different kinds of settlement schemes under this first villagization effort. The policy formulated under the First Five Year Plan states that villages were to be created in underpopulated regions of the country, that settlers would be recruited from economically underdeveloped areas, and that the government would provide planning, housing, water, and other support services in order to transform traditional farming practices. However, the actual experience of villagization was more diverse in implementation than design, and many settlements did not follow the guidelines laid down in the plan. There were both modernized old and new villages, settlements for food crop producers and cash crop producers, state farms and spontaneous rural reorganization.

While the social and economic organization of villages varied immensely, their technological foundations were strikingly similar. In his inaugural address to Parliament, Nyerere drew upon World Bank philosophy and his own social theory to explain the contours of the new program of agricultural mechanization. Nyerere very skillfully integrated a logic of technical improvements with social change:

> If we want to develop, we have no choice but to bring both our way of living and our way of farming up to date. The hand-hoe will not bring us the things we need today. Very often it has not even sufficed to bring us enough to eat. We have got to begin using the plough and tractor instead. But our people do not have enough money, and nor

has the Government, to provide each family with a tractor. So what we must do is try and make it possible for groups of farmers to get together and share the cost and the use of a tractor between them. But we cannot even do this if our people are going to continue to live scattered over a wide area, far apart from each other.

The first and absolutely essential thing to do, therefore, if we want to be able to start using tractors for cultivation, is to begin living in proper villages.[6]

Mechanization became the predominant technical input whatever the particular characteristics of individual experiments in village settlement. Following Nyerere's lead, the National Executive Committee of the Tanzanian African National Union (TANU) called for the introduction of mechanized farming, and the minister of agriculture described Tanzania's mechanization policy as predominantly a policy of tractorization. In 1963 Tanzania purchased 373 tractors and in the following year another 300. The credit for tractor purchases was channeled through the National Development Credit Agency (NDCA), which was set up in 1964 to lend capital to cooperative unions. These loans supported either agricultural mechanization or tobacco farming.[7]

The Lake District became the most important region of Tanzania for the implementation of a program of agricultural mechanization. The largest single recipient of tractors was the Victoria Federation of Cooperative Unions (VFCU) in Sukumaland.[8] In 1963 the VFCU received 168 tractors; in 1965, 85; in 1966–67, 148.[9] A tractor department was created within the cooperative at its head office in Mwanza. This office was responsible for monitoring the expenses and operations of the primary cooperative societies and for the day-to-day operations of tractor teams. Local agricultural extension provided technical advice to those farmers who participated in the agricultural schemes utilizing mechanization. TANU was responsible for recruiting settlers. In the Lake District, resettlement came in the form of block farms. Block farms were simply the aggregation of small-scale holdings into large-scale "blocks," to monocrop cotton, an important cash crop.

Block farms at their peak accounted for 5,000 settlers. Those farmers most interested in the scheme had been the landless and local elites, whose farms were made a part of block cultivation in a way that did not entail any alteration of tenure or status. It was expected that with increased technological inputs—mechanization was complemented by the use of pesticides and other technical supports—yields would be in the neighborhood of 540 kilograms per hectare. In fact, they were under 200, and thus very similar to those obtained by small-scale holders not participating in the agricultural mechanization program available to block farmers.[10] In the third year of operation many block farms closed down and small-scale holders slowly returned to the use of ox cultivation and to intercropping cotton with other crops. By 1968 there were no block farms anywhere in the country, and according to a working paper prepared for the formulation of the Second Five Year Plan, "the bulk order tractors as a whole can be expected by final repayment dates, to show a repayment of principal of about 35% only."[11]

The village settlement program was terminated on the recommendation of an external policy advice and evaluation mission, just as it was begun by one. A British mission in 1965 determined that the program was not paying for itself and should be discontinued. As was the case for block farms, production increases on settlement projects were in general no greater than those of traditional peasant agriculture. In April 1966, Vice President Kawawa called for an end to village settlement for which there were high capital investments or long-distance population movements. It was not a repudiation of villagization per se, but a change of economic and technical direction. According to Rene Dumont, one of the major reasons for the failure of village settlement was an overreliance on mechanization.[12] What made mechanization an inappropriate technology in the context of village settlement?

In the first place, the individual schemes were not carefully planned or monitored. There was no determination of whether the technology could be supported by the local production systems and infrastructure. This was the case because the scope of the program exceeded the capabilities of the institutions involved to plan and execute it. Village settlement, as pursued immediately after independence, was a pilot project of from five to eight villages. With the writing of the First Five Year Plan, the program was expanded to sixty-nine settlement schemes budgeted at £150,000 each. At the same time, two-thirds of the European agricultural officers who served during the colonial period left.[13] The Tanzanian Ministry of Agriculture (MOA) lamented that, though work was begun to recruit additional staff for the implementation of the first plan, it met "with little success at higher levels."[14] In 1963 the Village Settlement Agency was unable to locate even a minimal number of professionals to begin operations.[15] On top of this, the MOA was split into the Ministry of Agriculture, Forestry, and Wildlife, which was responsible for improvement agriculture, and the Ministry of Lands, Settlement, and Water Development, which implemented transformation agriculture. The bifurcation of the MOA, according to an FAO technical assistant, "led among other things to competition for scarce technical resources."[16]

Secondly, the repair and maintenance of machinery had not been adequately addressed. In many regions, there was simply no technical infrastructure. Tanzania did not have the technical capabilities to test tractors as did the agricultural engineering research station in Kenya. Of the thirty-eight businesses listed in the early sixties as engineering and repair services, only five fixed agricultural machinery.[17] These businesses were located primarily in the major cities, which greatly limited their accessibility. The local cooperatives, which were asked in many cases to shoulder the responsibility for repair, had previous to village settlement been primarily concerned with the marketing of crops. Thus, there was no cooperative tradition of technical repair. As in the case of the lack of technical personnel, the scarcity of such technical support was a direct inheritance of colonialism. The technical infrastructure in a human and material respect was simply not in place for a nationwide effort at technology transfer.

Thirdly, the use of mechanization was a very expensive vehicle for village settlement and transformation agriculture because of the status quo organization of production. The most common form of settlement was a stationary but highly diffused one, with a pattern of landholdings that was disaggregated. It was this organization of production that government administrators interested in agricultural mechanization attempted to address. Tanzania had the choice to mechanize only large-scale holders or, in other words, those forms of agricultural production that could clearly support the use of the technology. It could, in contrast, attempt to encourage a change in the organization of production among subsistence or cash crop farmers who cultivated crops on small-scale holdings. It pursued both strategies, but it was the latter that increased the cost of the program as whole.

In the Lake District, TANU worked to bring about change in the basic economic organization of production. From the beginning, those farmers most interested in settlement had been the landless and local elites. For those farmers who were not landless but who were also not larger-scale holders, the costs of monocropping and cooperative cultivation appeared high. In those areas like Sukumaland, where the state made a concerted effort to aggregate holdings, the mechanization program ran into resistance and sabotage from farmers interested in the technology but disinterested in greater dependence upon the state. In the first year of the program, an assistant field officer's house was burned down, and various other forms of explicit resistance continued throughout the program. Ultimately this impeded the continuation of the program.

Fourthly, the intrusion of governmental administration into the economic affairs of peasant cultivators did not have a salutary effect upon the receptivity of settlers to the requests made for change. In the day-to-day running of village settlement schemes, settlers were overridden by government officials on questions of how farms should be run and what was economical and what was not.[18] There was an administrative high-handedness in the role of the government in the new settlements. In many cases, settlement schemes were introduced into regions not hitherto consulted, and tractors shipped to cooperatives that were not prepared for their arrival. Further, besides the inattention to local needs and interests, party officials and government administrators used the new technology to further their own political fortunes, rather than those of the farmers they were to be servicing. According to the report of the Presidential Special Committee of Enquiry into the Co-operative Movement and Marketing Boards;

> Tractors financed with the Union borrowing from the National Development Credit Agency have been commandeered by Regional and Area Commissioners and operated at substantial losses for the benefit of non-co-operative schemes, sometimes, for example, required to be used on TANU Youth League Farms without charge. In a number of areas the local political leaders have commandeered the tractors, set up their own committees to determine tractor rate, decided who shall have use of the tractors and fixed the terms of credit on which they could be hired—even though it was the co-operative which incurred the financial liability for the tractors.[19]

The new state, uncertain about its political direction, was experimenting with the integration of politics and technics. Which constituencies were most important? How should they be made a part of the state? Who would need to make the sacrifices necessary for the modernization of agriculture? In a way, Tanzania in the early sixties wanted to have its cake and eat it too. The state moved to appeal to the rural gentry—small-scale cash crop farmers—and offer them a valuable new resource, and at the same time hoped that they would serve as a vanguard for the kind of social and economic change it wished to institute. This appeal was not well considered, because such changes would undermine, not accentuate, the economic and political power of this group. With the termination of settlement and widespread mechanization, cooperative unions, a private base of power for cash croppers, were reorganized by the state and never regained the power and autonomy that they enjoyed before they were made responsible for agricultural mechanization schemes. This seemed to indicate that the state was beginning to reconsider its choice of constituency. Perhaps all peasants were not alike? And, if this was the case, should the state do something about it? Tanzania was not yet sure. Both the initial resistance it met and the costliness of the technical vehicle led Nyerere to reconsider both his political and technical policies.

In 1966, at the time that Tanzania was reconsidering the wisdom of tractorization and terminating its first village settlement program, an FAO agricultural engineer was posted to the Kenyan Ministry of Agriculture to assist in determining what the mechanization needs of the country were, in what ways they varied across crops and scale of operations, and how mechanization capabilities could be coordinated to serve a multiplicity of agricultural needs. As a special part of this mandate, the FAO expert was asked "to provide assistance and advice needed by African farmers who are taking over large-scale farms for the first time."[20] He was also asked to establish a service for the peasant cultivators whose agricultural needs were more broadly defined. While it was not necessarily the peasant cultivator who benefited, it was the establishment of this service that became the focus of his work.

British aid provided the capital for the purchase of the tractors for peasant cultivators—fifty tractors were acquired with £100,000—but it was the FAO that designed, supervised, and monitored the project. The FAO was responsible for tractor hire services (THSs) in other African countries as well as Kenya. The policy was one conceived to reach farmers who might not otherwise have the benefits of such technological resources. At the same time, in Kenya the new THS was to be run like a commercial enterprise.[21] Thus, there was a contradiction in the original conceptualization. On the one hand, it was to reach farmers who could probably not pay for the service—and thus needed subsidization—and on the other, it was not to be subsidized. This contradiction was resolved with the creation of a peasant wheat scheme in the Rift Valley. That scheme, like the settlement program in Tanzania, was to provide a large-scale economic basis for peasant agriculture, and thus would make the use of the new technology economical. However, as in the case of Tanzania, the new technology, and its introduction as a part of large-scale peasant agriculture, was a Trojan horse for something other than sound economic policy.

Kenyatta, unlike Nyerere, was not a philosopher or a creator of grand political visions. He was, however, a student of African traditional society, especially that of his own people. Many years prior to independence, Kenyatta explained his own view of political authority and how it related to the Kikuyu people. In *Facing Mount Kenya*, his anthropology of the Kikuyu, Kenyatta explains that the political loyalties of individuals within traditional societies were determined by family and clan.[22] This theory resulted in an understanding of political constituency that was much more limited in scope than that of Tanzania. First came, literally, Kenyatta's family and clan, then those of close Kikuyu advisors and the cliques within the tribe that were of economic and political importance, and finally Kikuyu of little status. A "widening-out of the family" resulted in the integration of economic and political elites from other tribes—Masai, Luo, Kalenjin—and the building of alliances with other groups through the coopting of selected representatives. Thus, at independence the new state was founded upon an understanding of political power according to which a hierarchical differentiation among groups was part of the natural order of things: there would be families of greater power and status and responsibility than others. State building was based on such a social foundation and proceeded according to a principle of networking, which resulted in economic and political alliances within and across tribal and ethnic groups. As a consequence, some class and ethnic groups won, and others lost.

TABLE 3.1. Size Distribution of Large Farms in Keyna, 1970

Size of Farms (hectares)	Number of Farms	% of All Farms	Estimated Total area (1000 hectares)	% of All Farmland
0–50	741	23.3	15	0.6
50–99	304	9.6	23	0.8
100–299	685	21.6	134	5.0
300–499	471	14.9	186	6.9
500–999	498	15.7	373	13.9
1,000–1,999	243	7.6	364	13.5
2,000–3,999	107	3.4	321	11.9
4,000–19,000	111	3.5	1,273	47.3
20,000 and over	15	0.5		
All sizes	3,175	100.0	2,690	100.0

SOURCE: Joel D. Barkan and John J. Okumu, eds., *Politics and Public Policy in Kenya and Tanzania* (New York: Praeger, 1979), p. 162.

The Rift Valley had long been the center of Kenya's wheat production, and as such a center of European agriculture. For much longer, it had been the territory across which the Masai traveled in their seasonal search for water and good range land. While European colonialism had divested the Masai of considerable territory, the tribe was still in possession of large areas of fertile agricultural land, which was used largely for traditional pastoral pursuits. Soon after independence, Kenyatta addressed the issue of the Rift Valley and the Masai. Kenyatta assured the Masai that their Rift Valley lands would be protected but insisted that they must be developed. Kenyatta explained that "since you have land, you must develop it. God has given you good land and good soil. If you co-operate with the Government, we shall help you to get machines to cultivate the land to grow good crops.[23]

The Masai Wheat Scheme was established to grow wheat on previously uncultivated land. It was also to provide the sound economic foundation for the operation of the new THS. In 1966 the THS cultivated 3,500 acres of wheat on Masai land with twenty-five THS tractors, and in 1968 and 1969, with the assistance of the entire fleet, 12,000 and 6,000 acres respectively.[24] It was this work on large-scale wheat farms that led a government assessment of public and private tractor hire services in the region to compare the THS favorably to other such efforts (see table 3.2)

TABLE 3.2.   Range of Tractor-Operating Costs in East Africa

	Sources					
	1	2	3	4	5	6
Number of tractors	133	109	11	50	50	5
Hours/tractor/year	530	603	843	1,020	1,128	1,500
Running costs sh./hour						
Depreciation	6.30	6.45	4.48	10.34	6.64	4.00
Fuel and oil	5.60	4.67	4.57	6.70	6.65	6.32
Spares and repairs	2.93	2.93	5.30	6.53	6.52	1.71
Workshop/mechanics	2.06	1.54				
Wages	6.21	4.55	2.39	8.63	10.35	2.00
SUBTOTAL	23.10	20.14	16.74	32.20	30.16	14.03
Overhead sh./hour						
Supervision	6.54	6.48	4.20			2.86
Transport	1.00	0.67	—	4.56	3.98	—
Administration	1.38	2.61	2.53			—
SUBTOTAL	8.92	9.76	6.73	4.56	3.98	2.86
TOTAL COSTS sh/hr	32.02	29.90	23.47	36.76	34.14	16.89

SOURCE: Republic of Kenya, *Report of the Working Party on Agriculture Inputs* (Nairobi, 1971), p. 28.
1. Uganda: Tractor hire service, 1965; 2. Uganda: Mixed-group farms and hire service, 1965; 3. Kenya: Mwea-Tebere irrigation scheme, 1963–64; 4. Kenya: Tractor hire service, 1967–68; 5. Kenya: Tractor hire service, 1968–69; 6. Kenya: Private contractor, 1964.

The FAO was pleased that in the first two years of operation the THS made a profit.[25] And the agricultural engineer in charge believed the Kenyan THS was lucky to be operating on such a large-scale project.[26]

In striking contrast was the reaction of the Masai to the scheme. In 1968, the Narok District agricultural officer recounted the extent of Masai dissaffection with the government's development project:

The formation of Wheat Development Authority and its agent Masai Agricultural Development Organization without involving or putting the Masai in the picture in any stage of its formation aroused a lot of suspicion among the Masai and thus they stopped the operation of MADO on the 24th of May, and this continued until its dissolution of the 10th of July.[27]

A Kenyan administrator, several years after the formal termination of the program, explained that the government was aware "that the traditional attitude of the people, the level of development and political influences were also bound to have strong bearings on the success or failure of the THS."[28]

While traditional attitudes were undoubtedly initially strong, the political influences were primary. The government created a program which was run by the government for the Masai. The intervention of the state into the economic activities of the Masai was seen as the intervention of Kikuyu interests into those of the Masai. It was the Kikuyu who had been migrating into the Rift Valley for generations in search of land. It was the Kikuyu who now owned many of the large-scale European farms. The greatest threat was that, with the creation of this government wheat scheme, the Masai might lose the land upon which it was run. The government would, in some form, make a long-term claim upon the land, as well as upon the activity. Or, as in the Ngong area of Masailand, the registration of land to individual Masai cultivators would result in the immediate sale to Kikuyu.[29] So the Masai rejected the scheme and the government's tractors to prevent any changes in the social relations of production and went on to run their own wheat production supported by private contractors. The majority of Masai were not interested in alliance politics because they believed that the introduction of a new mode of production would result in the displacement of their right to exploit, as well as the means by which they exploited, Rift Valley lands. They had reason to fear the land hunger of the Kikuyu.

Along with the Masai Wheat Scheme, the THS was asked to cultivate cotton in Nyanza and Western provinces—Luo and Luhya regions of the country. As in the case of the Masai, these were ethnic communities with which the Kikuyu competed. But in this case, the competition was not for land, but for the investment of government resources in the development of local economies. The THS was never very active in meeting those needs. According to government regional reports, the THS did not actually work in Nyanza Province at the time of the FAO project, and between 1967 and 1968, the early years of the service, it did not venture into Western Province.[30] The FAO found that cotton was not an important crop to mechanize. Technically, it argued, the real limits on production were not in the preparation of the seed bed but in weeding and harvesting.[31] Furthermore, it discovered that it was terribly difficult in general to support the mechanization of small-scale farms, because it was not possible "to organize work systematically," and thus cover the costs of cultivation.[32] But at the same time, the THS was active in the Nyeri district of Central Province—not part of the formal mandate of the new service—where it provided assistance to mostly large-scale but some small-scale wheat farmers. Most of these farmers had no previous experience in farming and were in danger of not surviving economically.[33] Meeting the needs of small-scale holders in such a province could not have been different than meeting the needs of small-scale holders in the West in respect to the organization of production, but the infrastructure was much more extensive. And more importantly, the political economy was distinctly different: Nyeri district of Central Province was Kikuyu.

This pattern of resource allocation continued into the seventies. Long after the formal termination of the participation of the FAO, the government continued to offer a technical justification for the operations of the THS, while utilizing it in a highly political fashion. The service was not much larger in 1975–76 than it had been in 1965–66. Composed of fifty-four 60–70 horsepower tractors—six units of nine tractors each—it cultivated sugar cane, rice, groundnuts, cotton, wheat, and maize. The work program for that year called for the plowing, harrowing, and planting of crops in several provinces. As in the previous decade, the largest commitments were made to the Rift Valley and Nyanza and Western provinces.[34] The actual work accomplished was greatly at variance with this plan. 2,114.91 hectares were cultivated in Central Province, 1,707.21 in the Rift Valley, 1,053.10 in Nyanza Province, and 710.51 in Western Province. What these figures illustrate is that the THS met the needs of the rural African elite and the most important Kikuyu settlement schemes. Despite the high hectarage attributed to some Luo regions, the THS probably did not work many Luo farms. For example, according to district reports, the THS rarely visited the South Nyanza district.[35] And the paucity of THS support in Western Province in 1975–76 was preceded by a year in which the government had promised two units, or in other words twelve tractors. Only three tractors arrived.[36] The THS was simply more accessible to some communities and some classes than to others.

In the first five years of the operation, the THS lost 868,750 Ksh.[37] Despite its profits in the first two years, once the Masai Wheat Scheme was terminated, it became a public service which was largely subsidized by the government. The FAO found that "the normal protectiveness associated with civil service and lack of responsibility to Government, leads to a languid attitude which makes the operation of a commercial type venture difficult.[38] The government, in theory, saw its primary task as making the hire service as economically efficient as possible. In later years, there were no public records kept to document the farms worked or the charges levied. And in practice, as had been the case in Tanzania, a government tractor program rather quickly became a way to support the social relations of production that the government wished to introduce and to maintain the constituency to which it was most committed.

During the same year in which the first FAO expert worked with the Ministry of Agriculture on a national mechanization policy, the World Bank sponsored a policy advice and evaluation mission on agricultural mechanization. While dismayed by the costs of government-sponsored tractor pools, the Bank was impressed with "the continuing pressure from politically potent small-scale farmers for such a pool to be established," and determined that "a fairly rapid increase in the numbers of mechanical equipment is almost inevitable."[39] In order to make the integration of the tractor into Kenyan peasant agriculture economically viable and to strengthen the private sector, the Bank developed a credit program to transfer the technology directly to small-scale holders.

Credit for the purchase of tractors was made a part of the World Bank's Smallholder Agricultural Credit Project.[40] It was addressed to the farmer with from three to ten acres of land. The Bank hoped to reach 8,000 farmers with its project, which included credit for livestock, general crop development, and poultry, as well as tractors. The project's purpose was stated as supporting the development of Kenya's high-potential areas, the further consolidation of landholdings, and the introduction of private tenure. The regional focus of the project was, however, in Nyanza and Western provinces. In the first year of its operations, of the 210 tractors purchased, 144 were acquired by farmers in these two regions.[41] This would seem, in a political respect, to compensate for the regional focus of the THS. But the credit program was a failure, and the Bank refocused its project on farmers in the Rift Valley.

After five years of operation, 55.0 million Ksh had been lent to Kenyan farmers under the auspices of the Bank's Small Holder Agricultural Credit

Project. Only 4.5 million Ksh, 9 percent of the total, was lent to farmers for tractor purchases.[42] Tractor loans were not within easy reach of many farmers. And the World Bank's credit was, in many cases, offered to and accepted by farmers who had no previous experience with large-scale mechanization or large-scale loan obligations. Instead of the rapid diffusion of technology into the small-scale sector, many tractors were repossessed and loan payments deferred. By 1971, in Nyanza Province, only one farmer was interested in acquiring credit for the purchase of a tractor. Repayment of the loans was in general poor, and five tractors had in that year been repossessed.[43]

There were two primary sets of factors that explained the lack of success in the introduction of tractors into peasant agriculture in these provinces. The first concerned the lack of infrastructure. The repair and maintenance of the new technology was a continuing problem with which the farmers were unable to cope.[44] This was both an issue of the technology market and of the level of technical expertise of the farmers. The market conditions constrained farmers in their efforts to repair the machinery they had acquired. According to one analyst on the scene;

> There are too many agencies selling too many different makes of tractors and farm machinery. This fragmentation of business makes it impossible for many of the suppliers to obtain a sufficient volumne of business to be able to provide adequate parts and service to the customer, and has the effect of increasing overall machinery costs.[45]

At the same time, the level of supportive services in these regions was not as great as in some others. And, existing service shops were very often in the largest towns, not necessarily in close proximity to the users. This would not have been such a serious problem if the average African peasant farmer had been familiar with the repair of his own machine. But he was not, and the technical expertise available was not within easy reach. A training program for tractor operators was established at Narosurra, in the Rift Valley, with aid from the government, Oxfam, a British nongovernmental aid agency, and Denmark.[46] The government also eventually established a special mechanization extension unit, but its staff was largely concerned with supervising the THS. Neither of these services were well placed to serve farmers in the west and in general there were few such technical experts on the district level in touch with local farmers.[47]

The second major factor that prevented the mechanization loans from successfully diffusing the technology was a question of the organization of production. Small-scale peasant farmers could not support the credit they received with the production of the crops they grew. Both government and international agency observers found that the tractors were underutilized. The revenue to be earned on small-scale farms simply did not support the technology. And, in the western provinces, there was not enough work to be done on other farms or perhaps not enough experience on the part of operators to do the available work. In theory, the owner could provide mechanization services to other farmers, and with such income pay off the loan. The World Bank changed the regional direction of the second phase of the Small Holder Agricultural Credit Project in order to address this problem. Fifty percent of its mechanization loans now went to farmers in the Rift Valley, who were on the borders of settlement schemes or large-scale farms on which tractor cultivation was needed and could, in theory, be supported.[48] A larger scale of operations was needed to make the technology transfer viable. But the change of regional focus reflected a political as well as an economic logic.

In the late sixties, a political crisis of some magnitude erupted in the political relations of the Luo and the Kikuyu. The Luo began to align themselves with Kikuyu political leaders critical of the land transfer program. It was now clear to many that the landless were permanently locked out of the access to cultivatable land. In the midst of this growing confrontation, Tom Mboya was assassinated. Mboya had been a bridge between the economic and ethnic insiders and outsiders. The frustration and anger that led to Mau Mau in the 1950s was rekindled and led to an intensification of the opposition's efforts to gain the government's attention and to spontaneous protests in the west. The extension of government resources in the form of THS services and World Bank loans to the western provinces was cut off. It had been part of the state's alliance-building efforts, but with the dissaffection of the elites whom it had hoped to coopt, those resources were redirected to the Kikuyu strongholds of Central Province and the Rift Valley. The tractor was being transferred to those farmers upon which the state could depend—to those groups uninterested in social revolution—and upon which it was building its political structure.

Kenya sought, like Tanzania, to use the tractor to alter tenure relations where it could and to backstop those it had changed through other means.

As in the case of Tanzania, the tractor was an especially attractive instrument for this task. For the Rift Valley wheat scheme it could be used to invade Masai territory and impose a new economic and social order. Tractors could be driven in, operated independently of the Masai, and utilized to grow a new and valuable crop. In the case of the African rural elite, the tractor could be used to maintain their large-scale holdings. The utilization of the service could be justified economically in respect to these farms and thus in respect to these farmers. In this way, the technology was first employed to extend the gains of the rural gentry and later to maintain them. The THS was also sent to service the needs of an ethnic constituency as well as a class structure. It was subsidized most heavily in those regions of the country where Kikuyu farmers could be found and, in fact, where they demanded that the government meet their development needs. In other regions and in respect to other peoples, the government pursued a policy of benign neglect. Thus, while the tractor was used to impose a rural social relations of production in Kenya as had been the case in Tanzania, it was done so less extensively. The technical supports needed to maintain the program were for this reason much narrower, and the political, economic, and technical costs were substantially less.

Small-Scale Technology and Social Justice

The introduction of the ox plow and the creation of small-scale technology research programs were undertaken in both Tanzania and Kenya because of challenges to the status quo approach to development. Despite the fact that the two countries were going in very different directions—one socialist, the other capitalist—the challenges were quite similar. They were made in the name of the small-scale, independent producer whose interests appeared to be eclipsed by both states' development strategies. Tanzania confronted the call for a change in policy earlier than Kenya and dispensed with it more quickly, moving on to a more powerful statement of its communitarian goals and an even more ambitious program of tractorization. Kenya sidetracked the intent of the new projects but never fully rejected them. Both Kenya's and Tanzania's internal challengers were supported by international assistance agencies, themselves in the throes of a reconsideration of their own policy directions. However, none of these agencies effectively cooperated with each other on joint programs of mechanization research or careful project design, implementation, and follow-up. And thus, ultimately, they failed to have the intended impact.

In 1967, on the heels of the development failures of the early sixties, Tanzania formally declared its commitment to a change in development direction. The Arusha Declaration, the first public document on the nature of Tanzanian socialism, incorporated Nyerere's social democratic values with an explicit concern for the material basis of ujamaa. It differed most dramatically from Nyerere's earlier explanations of ujamaa in the attention it directed to economic development. The fraternity about which Nyerere had written so eloquently in the early sixties was now primarily a matter of the responsibility of the society for its own economic welfare. The conceptual axis on which the declaration swings is the idea of self-reliance. Self-reliance is economic sacrifice, hard work, and commitment to the eradication of poverty and economic underdevelopment. At the top, the party is asked to forego immediate economic gain, and limitations are placed on property ownership. At the bottom, the people are asked to work hard, take initiative in production, and recognize the limits of the state's economic capabilities.[49]

As a consequence of this new principle of self-reliance, the economic development of the country was to be highly focused in respect to the investment of scarce resources, both economic and technological. The Second Five Year Plan differs from the first in the sharp distinction it draws between peasant agriculture—the people—and highly capitalized state farms. There was to be no repeat of the mistakes of transformation agriculture. One sector, owned and operated by the state for the purposes of the cultivation of export crops and the earning of national revenue, would be the target of technological modernization and capital investment. According to the new plan, state farms were to be at the center of government investment in irrigation, mechanization, and other technology.[50] In contrast, the formation of villages and the promotion of change in peasant agriculture would involve little or no capital investments. Villagers were said to need "ideological and organizational" help, not material investment.[51] Development in peasant agriculture would result from the popular commitment of the masses of Tanzanians to the concerns of the new self-reliance.

A new direction in agricultural technology policy was outlined by Nyerere in the late sixties. The ox plow and small-scale technology became the symbol of the new self-reliance in respect to peasant agriculture.[52] Small-scale technology would prevent the growth of classes—maintain the egalitarian nature of African society—and preserve traditional values. It would allow the peasant himself to become self-reliant, to be responsible for his own modernization. Small-scale technology bridged the gap between traditional and modern society, at the same time that it joined traditional and modern agriculture. The moral imperatives that had been a part of Nyerere's early conception of ujamaa had not been eclipsed by the Arusha Declaration's material focus and were in fact preserved in this new technology program.

Nyerere's new view on technology and development, the reorientation of resource investment under the Second Five Year Plan, and the articulation of the Arusha Declaration were in part a consequence of the failure of village settlement, in part a consequence of the beginning of an internal debate on social revolution, and in part a consequence of external advice and evaluation. There was widespread consensus on the need to avoid further settlement development disasters. It was a time in Tanzania of policy reconsideration and redesign. Perhaps the most important external influence in a technical respect was the advice offered by E. F. Schumacher on the adoption of intermediate technology. Schumacher defined the need for gradual social and technical change based on the economic and human resources found in peasant society. Schumacher's consultation also opened the way for the negotiation of a new kind of ITDG/ILO technology project.

Immediately after the initiation of the Second Five Year Plan, in 1969, a joint ITDG/ILO mission was sent to Tanzania and Zambia to consider opportunities for the establishment of intermediate technology projects.[53] The ILO had just begun its World Employment Program and was relying upon Schumacher's contacts to begin its own efforts. The 1969 mission consulted with the Tanzanian Ministry of Regional Administration and Rural Development; the Ministry of Agriculture, Food, and Cooperatives; the Ministry of Commerce and Industry; and the Ministry of Economic Affairs and Development Planning. They visited a sisal estate, one ujamaa village—as successful resettlement efforts were now called—a handicrafts training center, a Chinese implements factory, and a few other associated institutions. The project drawn up as a result of their tour of the country and of their conversations with national officials included provision for one agricultural engineer, one economist, and one expert on intermediate technology. The agricultural engineer would work at the Tanzanian Agricultural Machinery Testing Unit (TAMTU) to assist in the design and production of prototypes and to help carry out an advisory service for rural craftsmen. The economist was to undertake feasibility studies on proposed equipment design, determine the marketability of these products, and advise the government in general on income and employment questions. The technology expert would establish an information center within the Ministry of Regional Administration and Rural Development on technologies available within and outside the country and was to organize demonstrations at rural training centers. While the Ministry of Economic Affairs and Development Planning was very interested in the project, the mission concluded that the success of this project would depend "largely upon the vigour with which it is promoted by the responsible officials within the Ministry of Rural Development."[54]

There was enough consensus within the government on the importance of the project that the UNDP was urged to support it. There was a year's delay between the negotiation in late 1969 and its acceptance as a part of the UNDP's budget in 1970. It was actually begun in 1971. Given that the country was still considering the direction it would take in respect to socialism and rural development, the gap between when the project was accepted and when it was initiated was big enough to sink it. Two experts were finally supported. The Ministry of Regional Administration and Rural Development had opted out of any commitment to the new technical direction. By 1971 the government was reconsidering the the role of agricultural mechanization in rural development, and as one UN official so delicately put it, the economist "was simply there at the wrong time."[55] The agricultural engineer, who had the largest impact, would himself write; "On taking up his duties, the expert found that a new orientation had been given to his assignment and that only a few guidelines had been laid down."[56]

Even though the agricultural engineer arrived in Tanzania to find that "a new orientation had been given to his assignment," he made the theories of both Nyerere and Schumacher on small-scale technology the basis of his work at TAMTU. Establishing a special section on intermediate technology, the expert over the course of a three-year period designed a variety of workshop tools for village carpentry and blacksmithing; transport equipment—wheelbarrows, a donkey cart, an ox cart; and agricultural implements including two types of harrows, a hand-operated planter, a fertilizer applier, and an ox- or donkey-drawn cultivator with harness. This type of work was not new to TAMTU. As a part of the early sixties' Three Year Plan TAMTU was allocated £23,000 to continue work on small-scale farming equipment, and £45,000 was set aside for the improvement of subsistence farming practices—specifically for the purchase of ox carts, cultivators, harrows, and ridging plows. And it was TAMTU that had been given the primary mandate in the Second Five Year Plan to promote small-scale technology. In the mid-sixties, it remained interested in the development of a small ox-drawn tool bar, and it undertook tests on all varieties of ox-drawn farm machinery.[57] However, while not unusual in the context of TAMTU, the ITDG/ILO expert's work was unique in the following respect. The expert strove to incorporate resources in his designs that were easily accessible to the average Tanzanian, including wood, goatskin, old bicycle frames, parts of old cars, and other scrap metal. He was also concerned with the final cost of his technologies. The ox cart that TAMTU was at the time manufacturing was, at its cheapest, Tsh 710, while the ITDG/ILO engineer's was Tsh 335. Given the villager's average yearly income of about Tsh 657, a savings of Tsh 375 was of considerable economic importance.[58]

Besides carrying out his work as an agricultural engineer, the ITDG/ILO expert attempted to popularize the notion of intermediate technology in Tanzania. He helped to establish village workshops and led training courses for village farmers. He spent a great deal of his time peddling his ideas on village technology to government officials, including regional authorities, and was successful in having his project covered by local media. He also wrote a book that set out his designs.[59] Two small pamphlets, which are excerpts from that book, have been published in Swahili. In essence, the expert went to great lengths to exploit the avenues open to him to get his ideas across. He believed that his job was to transfer knowledge as well as technology. Wanting to contribute in some small way to the villager's own technological self-reliance, he sought to use both direct and indirect methods to do so.

The ITDG/ILO project was not the only effort to introduce small-scale technology into peasant agriculture. German assistance provided TAMTU with production as well as research capability in the area of small-scale technology. The government supported this work, subsidizing the sale of ox carts. The Chinese extended a loan to construct a farm implements manufacturing concern. There was also government support for agricultural extension and the introduction of small-scale technology into cultures in which the use of animals and animal power was an innovation.

There is considerable controversy over the success of these efforts. On the one hand, in some parts of the country, oxen given to villages for cultivation purposes were slaughtered. Even with government subsidization, the TAMTU ox carts were actually too expensive for peasant farmers. And the work of the ITDG/ILO expert was seen as highly idiosyncratic. On the other hand, the demand for ox carts was so great that TAMTU's production unit could not keep up with the requests for carts. The revenue from the sale of carts went from Tsh 19,086.30 to Tsh 112,158.95 in a matter of a few years.[60] Some analysts have determined that the extension back-up for the program of technology development was underfunded and underimplemented.[61] The ITDG/ILO project itself did not entail the kind of resource investment that had been originally planned.

If the small-scale technology work of this period is judged a failure by national or international policymakers, it must, however, be so judged because of the dramatic shift in the political winds of change which were sweeping through Tanzania in the late sixties and early seventies. With the collapse of the village settlement program, the fate of ujamaa in the rural areas hung in the balance. There was considerable disagreement on how to proceed in respect to the introduction of socialism to Tanzanian peasants. Regional authorities were given responsibility for villages. Some regional authorities took no action at all, others attempted to secure government resources as incentives, and still others used coercion.[62] Nyerere's technology policy was an appeal to a voluntaristic and incremental approach. Step by step, new technology would be adopted, and step by step, social change would be effected. This perspective required a great deal of patience and a long-term time frame, something the state ultimately did not have. It also required a rather limited constituency. The focus on small-scale technology, given the size of the program and previous technical development, inevitably was addressed to the interests of progressive farmers. This presented problems for a country whose concern with social and economic equity was growing. There were no clear class delineations made in the Arusha Declaration, but at the turn of the decade, Tanzania had discovered class politics, and the race was on to promote economic and social equity at the expense of social differentiation.

At the same time that the Tanzanians were designing their new approach to development, Kenyan development policymakers, technical experts, and scholars met at Kericho to discuss how to prevent Kenya from confronting a future of "social injustice and conflict, of retarded economic growth, of misplaced values and aspirations."[63] Like the Tanzanian Arusha Declaration, the 1966 Kericho conference was populist in spirit and called for the country to build upon the energy, initiative, and leadership that resided within the community itself. Also, very much like the principles adopted at Arusha, the ideals set out at Kericho were the basis for an experimental effort at voluntary peasant development. Neither state would really transfer such economic power into the hands of the masses, but Kenya, like Tanzania, experimented with the possibility. Small-scale technology was part of that experiment largely because of the new technical direction set by international assistance agencies.

The next cycle of the World Bank's Small Holder Agricultural Credit Project included a request from the government for tractor loans.[64] Kenya argued that the number of tractors available to small-scale holders was quite limited and largely a function of whether the existing national pool of technology was in high or low demand in the large-scale sector. The government's assessment was, in fact, accurate in respect to peasant agriculture. In 1966, there were 6,438 tractors in Kenya, and only 500 of these worked in the small-scale farming sector.[65] In 1971 there were 5,000–5,500 tractors working on large-scale farms; 1,000–1,500 working in commercial transport, construction, and the small-scale farming sector; and 500 tractors under the supervision of the central and local governments.[66] However, the Bank questioned whether the best way to rectify the situation of the peasant farmer was with the continuation of the previous technology policy. As a part of its agricultural credit program, the Bank took a cautious stance and funded neither tractors nor ox cultivation. Instead it began a research effort through its Transportation and Urban Projects Department to determine in what ways agricultural and transportation equipment were complementary. It hoped to discover how such technologies were interchangeable and thus to be able to tailor future programs to meet the many needs of small-scale farmers. Did the tractor or animal draft best suit the variety of circumstances to which small-scale farmers were subject? The Bank provided assistance to Kenya Industrial Estates, a public corporation, to support the establishment of a local manufacturing capability in the area of small-scale technology. Thus, the Bank redefined its own lending policies and cautiously moved into the area of small-scale technology development.

This followed a reconsideration by the World Bank of its philosophy on development in general and on development in Kenya in particular. The Bank's new direction was shared as well by other major assistance actors. In 1971 just as the Kericho experiments were getting under way, the International Labor Organization sent a large policy advice and evaluation mission to Kenya as a part of its World Employment Program. Invited to do a complete evaluation of the employment problem in Kenya, the report was undiplomatic in the extreme.[67] The organization bluntly recommended that land be redistributed, large-scale holdings be dismantled, and that small-scale, labor-intensive farms be established as a basis for full employment. It identified the basic problem as structural in nature. The Bank also undertook a comprehensive assessment of the Kenyan economy in the early seventies. Congratulating Kenya on its high rate of national savings, the organization refrained from calling for a radical redistribution of wealth, but its economic policy recommendations also called for structural change.[68] Its major recommendations included, on the one hand, a reorientation of price policy, exchange rates, interest rates, and wage rates to reduce the level of government protection and subsidization, and on the other, an increase of investment in agriculture, labor-intensive industries, and small-scale enterprises.

In the midst of the Bank's renegotiation of agricultural credit and following the publishing of the ILO and Bank assessments, the FAO launched an appropriate technology project in the area of agricultural mechanization. In the spring of 1977 the FAO began an effort to increase the productivity of the small-scale farmer through the improvement of hand tools, ox equipment, and small-scale motorized technology.[69] The objectives of the project included research, extension, and manufacturing components, but the research program was primary. Like the World Bank, the FAO was interested in determining for itself what would work best in Kenya. However, as an agency, the FAO was not in agreement with the approach taken by either the ILO or the World Bank, and the project for which it was now responsible was distinctively its own.

The FAO expert assigned to Kenya had carried out similar research in England. He was the inventor of the "snail"—a wheel-mounted, power-driven winch with a cable to be used in pulling a plow or other simple equipment. Disdainful of the work of organizations like the ITDG, the expert saw small-scale technology research as an extremely complex venture, comparable to that done in respect to the tractor. In the course of the project, between 1977 and 1981, the FAO would test hundreds of technologies. The FAO expert and a Kenyan assistant determined that seven varieties of small-scale technology, some using animal draft, some relying upon human labor, best suited Kenyan circumstances.[70] However, the focus of concern at the beginning of the project was on the technical sophistication of technology, and many small-scale tractors were tested as well. This was done in part to meet the needs of a very different constituency—small-scale holders could afford neither a large- or small-scale tractor—but it was done primarily to satisfy the FAO's concern with the efficiency and capability of the new invention of its own expert. At the conclusion of its research, its determination that the snail might still be the best alternative to the tractor was of no surprise.

As originally planned, the FAO research project was to be located in the Eastern and Western provinces at technical institutes in Embu and Bukara. These are regions of the country where the use of animal draft and ox plows were already in use but not widely diffused. For the extension component of the FAO's work, it was thought important to locate the project in regions of the country where there was already a clientele. However, the government argued that the expert was best located in Nairobi at the Ministry of Agriculture. The Land and Farm Management Division of the MOA maintained a strong commitment to tractors.[71] Certain to be marginalized by the perspective of this department and in no direct contact with any research facilities, the FAO reached a compromise of sorts with the government, and the small-scale technology project was established at the government's testing and research unit at Nakuru in the Rift Valley. The Nakuru research and testing unit is almost entirely concerned with the testing of tractors and tractor equipment and was certainly not the best institution at which to locate appropriate technology research.[72] Nakuru is, of course, also located in the heart of the former White Highlands, and as such is in close proximity to the constituency the state is most interested in servicing. A Kenyan assistant was sent to Bukura in western Kenya, but he was later moved to Katumani in Eastern Province on the boundaries of new Kikuyu settlements and in the territory of ethnic constituencies with which the Kikuyu have strong alliances.

The FAO itself seemed ill advised as to the significance of its own project to a turnaround in development strategy. While aware of each other's work in the area of small-scale technology in Kenya, the ILO, the World Bank, and the FAO were not making any efforts to formally cooperate or complement one another's work. In fact, the ILO and the World Bank had duplicated each other's efforts in the area of policy advice and evaluation; and the World Bank and the FAO were both engaged in research projects into the problem of small-scale technology. Each saw its work in respect to the overall goals of the agency, rather than the overall condition of the country. The ILO was most concerned with employment, the World Bank with reaching the rural poor, and the FAO with technical modernization. Had they combined their collective resources and diplomacy, a project might have been sponsored that combined the planning capabilities of the ILO, the capital assistance of the World Bank, and the technical expertise of the FAO. This might have resulted in a project in which technologies were diffused as well as researched. The agencies might also have, as a consequence, been able to convince the Kenyan MOA of the importance of their work.

The questions of social justice and economic equity raised by the ILO and the World Bank reports made no impact upon the Kenyan MOA. Ox cultivation had been dismissed by the government in its requests to the World Bank for technology assistance as too dependent upon primitive local technology, as reducing employment possibilities, and as incurring high opportunity costs in areas where the grazing of animals took land out of cultivation. As one staff member explained, ox cultivation was no more a part of traditional peasant agriculture than was the tractor. Both had been introduced by Europeans, but one was simply better than the other. And yet, the government's resistance to small-scale technology was a resistance to the larger goals of the international assistance community and to the legacy of the Kericho conference. The Kericho conference had given birth to the Special Rural Development Program (SRDP). The SRDP was an attempt at structural change.[73] While it had the strong support of the then Ministry of Economic Planning and Development, it was ignored by other branches of the development bureaucracy that were important to its success. Thus, while the World Bank and the FAO could find support with the government's economic planners for the funding of small-scale technology research, they could not obtain the interest or commitment of the major decision makers or technicians. Like the SRDP, small-scale technology efforts would be marginalized, or if implemented, they would be directed to a community not generally characterized as a part of Kenya's rural poor.

The battle over small-scale technology had another layer of political significance as well. It was certainly part of a clash between two groups within the bureaucracy over planning goals and development aims—productivity versus employment and income. It was also a conflict over scale of production and symbolized the disagreement concerning the class basis of agricultural development. But, finally, and perhaps most importantly, it was a debate on whose technical and cultural traditions mattered most. The Luo and other western peoples had widely adopted ox technology; the Kikuyu had not. Beyond the question of class, the small-scale farmers most important to the state did not embrace a tradition of animal draft. Thus, the development of a small-scale technology program was the development of a program that drew on the experience and the needs of the peoples of the western part of the country. In this respect, small-scale technical development, like large-scale technical development, was part of the high politics of ethnic conflict and thus at the center of the state's definition of its political constituency.

Technical Innovation as Social Revolution

By the middle of the seventies, the emphasis of Kenya's agricultural development program was more and more in the direction of genetic improvements in crops and the development of high-yielding varieties. For Tanzania, however, agricultural mechanization, and especially the tractor, retained an attraction with which few other forms of agricultural technology could compete. In 1971 a new set of party guidelines were drawn up which replaced the Arusha Declaration. The Mwongozo Guidelines gave TANU unquestioned responsibility for leading a social revolution from above. Fraternity, self-reliance, and the values of traditional society were eclipsed by the necessity of protecting the people from imperialism, preventing economic exploitation, and keeping neocolonialism at bay.[74] National security was never mentioned, but protecting the security of the nation was what Mwongozo was all about. Hostile classes within and without Tanzania were working to undermine ujamaa. Anticipating a frontal assault, the state began a more intense program of villagization, or in other words, it rapidly stepped up the transformation of the rural social order. Ujamaa meant villages, cooperative cultivation, common ownership of property, and the end of the successful progressive farmer. The tractor once again became the technology of social change.

Regional authority was strengthened after the Arusha Declaration, and more and more responsibility was handed to local authorities for the investment of development resources. As a consequence, central technical authorities were weakened, while regional political authorities were given more power for technical decisions. In 1967 the Regional Development Fund was created, and in 1968 regional economic secretaries were appointed. At the same time, the Ministry for Rural and Regional Development had been placed directly under the office of the president. In the early seventies, six former cabinet members were made regional commissioners. All eighteen commissioners were then given ministerial status and began to serve on TANU's National Executive Committee.[75] At first, development decision making at the regional levels was dominated by the central government's technical experts and was under the supervision of the technical ministries.[76] The fund was, as a consequence, used strictly for agricultural development projects that were designed to increase production. Later, while many economic development projects remained the purview of technical ministries, others were placed directly under regional administration.[77] It was regional authority that oversaw a massive increase in large-scale mechanization for peasant agriculture.

While the Second Five Year Plan's overwhelming emphasis had been on small-scale technology, there had been one small equivocation on the subject of agricultural mechanization: "Where soundly based ujamaa or

TABLE 3.3.   Tractor Imports, 1960–1972

Year	Number of Tractors
1960	432
1961	313
1962	281
1963	846
1964	569
1965	612
1966	399
1967	520
1968	861
1969	750
1970	856
1971	693
1972	603

SOURCE: Adolfo C. Mascarenhas and Margaret Skutsch, *A Background to Rural Employment in Tanzania*, April (Geneva: ILO, 1976), p. 65.

co-operative production units are established, the opportunities for effectively utilizing tractors, as well as ox-powered equipment, will be carefully evaluated for appropriate crops."[78] The small equivocation in the plan became a major government program of agricultural mechanization. Initiated in a few regions in the late sixties, the policy was implemented nationwide in the early seventies. Approximately $32 million was spent on the import of agricultural machinery between 1969 and 1974, constituting 30 percent of agricultural development expenditures for both central and regional institutions.[79] Regional authorities began to supply tractors to villages in 1970, and between 1971 and 1974, the Tanzanian Rural Development Bank provided loans directly to ujamaa villages for tractors.[80]

This program of regionally supervised tractorization was undertaken to alter the pattern of villagization that resulted from the policies of the late sixties. Many cash crop areas like Morogoro, Mwanza, and Kilimanjaro were without villages (see table 3.4).[81] In other words, those regions in which the real economic power of the country resided did not embrace the idea of cooperative cultivation or ujamaa villages.[82] The acceleration of villagization in the early seventies again cast the net very wide in an effort to induct both rich and poor peasants into a national network of villages. Mechanization was central to this effort. No one bothered to correct for

TABLE 3.4. Stages of Development in Ujamaa Villages, 1970–1971

		Approximate Population		
	Number of Villages	Average per village	Regional total	Regional total as % of all regional population
Arusha	44	200	9,000	1.3
Coast	58	940	55,000	6.0
Dodoma	150	310	47,000	5.9
Iringa	350	240	84,000	10.8
Kigoma	108	300	32,000	6.3
Kilimanjaro	11	190	2,000	0.3
Mara	250	380	95,000	15.5
Mbeya	194	260	50,000	4.6
Morogoro	24	210	5,000	0.7
Mtwara	672	420	282,000	44.1
Linda	188	420	79,000	18.3
Mwanza	41	190	8,000	0.7
Ruvuma	120	100	12,000	2.7
Shinyanga	132	100	13,000	1.3
Singida	57	230	13,000	2.7
Tabora	82	240	20,000	3.2
Tanga	146	160	23,000	2.7
West Lake	43	250	11,000	1.5
Totals and Averages	2,668	315	840,000	6.3

SOURCE: Antony Ellman, "Group Farming Experiences in Tanzania," in Peter Dorner, ed., *Cooperative and Commune: Group Farming in the Economic Development of Agriculture* (Madison: University of Wisconsin Press, 1977), p. 246.

the earlier errors of the program of transformation agriculture and most of them were repeated. But this time, the technology transfer policy was a straightforward program of transferring peasants as well as technology. It did not work. The tractor was not a significant enough reason for independent cash croppers to join communal settlements. In 1973, 70 percent of the population in villages was still located in the five poorest regions of the country that together produced only 25 percent of the gross domestic product (GDP).[83] Villagization itself was becoming a residue of class differentiation. That same year Nyerere announced what was, in effect, mandatory villagization. The following year a policy of forced villagization began and party and army cadres were mobilized to move

TABLE 3.5. Ujamaa Villages, 1967–1974

Year	Number	Total Population	Average Population	Total Village Population as % of National Population
1967	48	5,000	104	0.04
1968	180	58,000	322	0.5
1969	809	300,000	371	2.5
1970	1,956	531,200	272	4.3
1971	4,484	1,545,240	345	12.3
1972	5,556	1,980,862	357	15.3
1973	5,628	2,028,164	360	15.3
1974	5,008	2,560,000	511	17.6

SOURCE: Antony Ellman, "Group Farming Experiences in Tanzania," in Peter Dorner, ed., *Cooperative and Commune: Group Farming in the Economic Development of Agriculture* (Madison: University of Wisconsin Press, 1977), p. 245.

those peasants who would not go willingly. As one Sukuma farmer candidly told an international technical assistant, "we would have slit their throats if we knew they were coming."[84] The FAO team that toured the country that year saw burned villages and crops. There had been a struggle, but the state and its vision of the new social order had prevailed, as did its new technology policy.

In 1974 the Tanzanian government requested assistance from the Food and Agriculture Organization for the reorganization and reconstruction of its mechanization capabilities. The FAO launched a policy advice and evaluation mission to assess the general context of agricultural mechanization—in other words, the consequences of the recent massive importation of tractors. Greeting the arrival of the FAO team was a desert of 3,000 unrepaired and inoperable tractors. The mission covered 6,000 miles and visited nine regions. It undertook a preliminary assessment of the cost of tractorization on the village level and concluded that, given the basic cost of the tractor, the maintenance and fuel costs, the lack of experienced staff, and the level of production, the technology was much too expensive a means for improving peasant agriculture. However, while they found the situation in respect to agricultural mechanization to be serious, even dire, the FAO team was impressed with the open and frank nature of their discussion with national officials. The mission concluded that for the Tanzanians, tractors were not simply pieces of machinery but agents of economic and social modernization, and as such, potentially extremely valuable tools of agricultural development:

It is the considered opinion of the members of the Mission, and of the great majority of the many Tanzanians who so willingly discussed mechanization with them, that a steady development of mechanization of agricultural operation is inevitable and that to come to conclusions and make recommendations solely on the basis of (capitalist) economic theory and cost-benefit studies may well be condemning as a failure a very bold experiment in the transformation of the lives of a nation which is desperately striving to lift itself into a new and better age.[85]

While not capitalist, Tanzania was firmly pro-tractor, and its approach to agricultural development was in strong agreement with the institutional bias of the FAO. The two were seemingly strange bedfellows in respect to economic theory, but in respect to technology choice, they could not have been better suited. Following the recommendations of the policy advice and evaluation mission, the FAO agreed to provide more field research into the general problem of Tanzanian agricultural mechanization needs. The FAO consultant who undertook the work agreed with the assessments of the general mission that large-scale mechanization was best suited to the work of state farms and other large-scale agricultural enterprises. The FAO consultant went so far as to suggest that the government consider other types of technology—piped water supplies, irrigation, electricity—as inducements to villagization and as recipients of government subsidization.[86] However, the agency went on to support a technical expert to advise the Ministry of Agriculture on a program of tractor restoration and the establishment of centers for the running, repair, and maintenance of tractor technology. In other words, the FAO was fully prepared to assist Tanzania in its policy of large-scale mechanization, despite its judgment that the technology did not suit Tanzanian circumstances.

The FAO proposed to resuscitate the tractors lying idle and create central workshops in which tractors would be repaired and maintained and from which they would be hired. A research project to determine the extent of disrepair was launched by the FAO in 1976. The field researcher who undertook the work determined that 2,000 of the 3,000 tractors might be restored to useful working order. But, despite this finding, the aid for the restoration program itself was slow in coming. The UNDP's financial crisis of the early seventies limited the FAO's access to capital, and the FAO technical assistant working with the Ministry of Agriculture began to lobby bilateral and multilateral donors for the necessary funds. A total of $80,600 was needed for a pilot resuscitation program, but according to the FAO "possible donors, in general, seem to be so obsessed with the unfortunate history of tractorization in Tanzania that the true remedial nature of current proposals is either not fully appreciated, or is disbelieved."[87] It was similarly difficult to find support for the FAO's proposed repair and maintenance centers. The FAO had intended to carry out field projects that would establish repair and maintenance shops in rural areas for tractors and other mechanization technology.[88] These centers were to undertake field testing, demonstration, and other extension activities and, in some instances, provide tractors for hire. The FAO saw these centers as a way to organize the mechanization of ujamaa villages where "the necessary managerial, organizational, operational, and technical skills are lacking."[89] The agency was unable to interest the World Bank in its projects. In 1977 a Swiss voluntary agency had contributed a small amount to the resuscitation program, and the FAO had begun to involve Italian aid in its repair and maintenance program.

Unable to enlist very extensive or enthusiastic support from other international agencies or from its own source of capital assistance—the UNDP—for its effort to provide a basis for large-scale mechanization in Tanzania, the FAO turned to the multinational corporations that had sold the technology. The head of the agency's Agricultural Engineering Service in Rome initiated a meeting between Tanzanian officials and the FAO's Industry Cooperative Program (ICP). This resulted in the extension of an invitation to various manufacturers of tractors—FIAT, Ford, Massey-Ferguson, John Deere, and Caterpillar—to visit the country and discuss the problem of tractorization. The government maintained that one of the primary reasons that tractor repair and maintenance had been such a problem was the unavailability of spare parts. Local distributors were simply not properly stocked. The tractor companies, however, stressed the necessity for the government and its agents to order the number and type of parts needed in advance of tractor breakdown. The companies blamed the state bureaucracy for the delay in orders and the late arrival of spare parts, while at the same time expressing uncertainty about their own long-term commitment to a country in which their businesses might be nationalized. The consequence of the ICP mission was that the companies agreed to offer limited training courses in repair and maintenance, while remaining aloof from the FAO's larger policy goals of restoration, repair, and maintenance.

Though committed to rebuilding Tanzania's mechanization capabilities through the mobilization of international aid and private investment, the FAO also hoped to trigger change in the development direction embraced by national officials. To begin with, the FAO was interested in reestablishing the authority of technical ministries, most specifically the Ministry of Agriculture. The rise of regional administration and its control of the mechanization program was identified by the FAO as the cause of a misguided mechanization policy. As the FAO consultant who carried out field research on the mechanization requirements of Tanzanian farmers recommended;

> Technical and financial considerations must be taken into account when specifying and operating equipment. These decisions can only be taken sensibly by competent specialists in this field, to whom senior administrators in overall control should turn for professional advice.
>
> Senior administrators should then defend all reasonable actions taken by their specialist mechanization staff on technical, logistic, management, and economic grounds. They should not yield to social pressures exerted on themselves or on junior officers by third parties for technical reasons.[90]

With the Ministry of Agriculture in control of agricultural mechanization, future programs would be carried out with full appreciation of the needs and limitations of the technology.

Beyond the question of technical versus political authority, there was, for the FAO, an issue as well of the eclipse of the private market. In general, many of the FAO personnel associated with the initial mission or with the monitoring of the project were uncomfortable with Tanzania's program of ujamaa. One member of the mission wondered whether large-scale mechanization could ever work as a catalyst of basic economic and social change. Another believed that the dislocation of the rural areas and the consequent confusion would hamper rural development for some time. An FAO staff member in Rome responsible for Tanzanian assistance projects explained that for an organization like the FAO it was difficult, particularly in the area of mechanization policy, to operate when the private sector was abolished. The FAO did not launch a frontal assault on the whole program of socialist villages, but it did hope to be able to convince the government to support small, privately operated contractors. These contractors were politically controversial, but for the FAO their work in Tanzanian agriculture was the model for the mechanization of the country as a whole. The FAO identified the small-scale contractor, who operated in the north and in the Lake District, as the genuine representative of Tanzanian technological self-reliance. These contractors were, of course, the progeny of decades of mechanization assistance of both a small scale and large variety in areas like Sukumaland. They were also the progressive farmers who resisted villagization.

The small-scale technology concerns of the policy advice and evaluation mission and the FAO researcher were never seriously pursued. The FAO knew that 75 percent of all land was still cultivated with the *jembe*—a short-handled hoe. It knew that while the use of the ox plow was common in some areas of the country, the use of other animal draft technology—tool bars, harrows, and planters—was not. It knew that animal draft technology would more adequately suit the constraints of peasant agriculture and move agriculture beyond hand hoe cultivation. The FAO technical assistant attempted to convince the government to impose a two-year moratorium on the importation of tractors. He also discussed with the World Bank the need for support for the relocation of TAMTU, the buying of imported hand tools, and the establishment of rural crafts centers with ox-training capabilities. But, in the main, the most serious efforts to mobilize aid and support were directed to the creation of a new foundation for large-scale mechanization. Essentially, the FAO believed that the tractor was the appropriate tool of agricultural modernization. If this assumption informs technology policy, then the findings of field research and a more complex understanding of Tanzanian farming systems, whatever their implications, will not reorient policy. In this respect, the political commitments of the FAO had the same impact on its technical programs that the state-building strategy of Tanzania had upon its technical direction.

The tractor focus of the seventies, it must be said, was largely the choice of Tanzania, not of the FAO or any other international assistance agency. Further, this was not a case of multinational corporations selling an innocent country a corrupt bill of goods. Tanzania had wide-ranging experience with tractorization and well understood the constraints to the utilization of this technology in peasant agriculture. But the impetus to the adoption of the technology was a powerful one. The state had decided to accelerate the pace of villagization in order to capture a wider constituency for its program of ujamaa. Once this decision was made, economic as well as political development resources were allocated by regional administrations to win hearts and minds. The tractor became the technology of peasant farming because the majority of Tanzanian peasants had become the prime target group of political development.

Yet tractorization did not work. In 1970, 531,000 Tanzanians were a part of villages. This figure represents 5 percent of Tanzania's mainland population. In 1974, after the period of economic incentives, 14 percent of the population had been villagized. This was rapidly increased to 60 percent following the use of force. By 1977, 79 percent of the mainland population—85 percent of the rural population—lived in government-created villages.[91] What the tractor had been unable to accomplish, the mobilization of party and military forces did. Why wasn't the ITDG or the ILO invited back to launch small-scale technology projects? The ITDG/ILO expert had exercised a certain well-informed understanding of the future in using old automobile parts to design small-scale technology. A tractor desert of 3,000 inoperative tractors would trigger a small-scale technology revolution. Though the introduction of the tractor did not result in a massive voluntary move into villages, it was now expected that it would help to maintain the new social order. Tractors, to be economical, needed large-scale agriculture. The cooperative cultivation, which was the aim of villagization, would be given a strong technological undergirding with large-scale mechanization. The use of improved hand tools or the ox plow simply could not compete as instruments of such agricultural collectivization. While the FAO might attempt to work for greater technical power and private contractors, the political handwriting had long been on the walls of the Ministry of Agriculture. State building would set the perimeters of economic and technical development.

The Technology of State Building and International Feudalism

By the second decade of its independent economic and political development, Tanzania had chosen its constituency. The country emerged from colonialism with a political legacy of uncertainty in respect to the social foundations of power. Who exactly had inherited the state? The British colonial administration had waffled between the idealism of mandate philosophy—native interests are protected—and the pursuit of economic change which resulted in the creation of a class of progressive, cash crop farmers. Nyerere was always most comfortable with an interpretation of African society and history that stressed the basic egalitarian nature of the social order. Or in other words, the state had an obligation to address the economic needs and political interests of the majority of the population. Independent economic development that might result in further social differentiation, more progressive farmers, and more landless farmers became the enemy of this obligation. Nyerere was an idealist, and he placed the long-term social basis of state power at the top of his political agenda. To insure equality, the state moved to protect the rights of the majority.

With such a constituency the state directed its economic-development resources to many regions, crops, farming systems, and farmers. It seriously attempted to meet the economic needs of the masses. It did this in part to garner legitimacy for state institutions and in part to extend its authority. Because its economic development aims were so highly diffused, it overtaxed its technical support system and introduced technology into production systems in which it was uneconomical. There were no repair and maintenance facilities in Tanzania to support the transfer of 3,000 tractors—no trained drivers, gasoline stations, transport facilities, agricultural extension programs, research and testing, or any other forms of infrastructural support. Britain had only meagerly developed the interior of the country, and there was no support system created after independence. Further, tractors were frequently sent into farming systems whose annual production could support neither the purchase nor the maintenance of such large-scale technology. Tanzania's technology transfer goals were ambitious, but its system of support was highly constrained.

The tractor was nevertheless a highly attractive technology choice. The tractor was used as a symbol of the state, as its concrete representation, and as an instrument of coercion. There was no other technological resource that was so popular: the tractor substituted its power for that of family labor and took much of the drudgery out of primary cultivation. There was also no other technological resource that made farmers as dependent upon the new institutions of the state. It was the state that provided credit, technical advice, and, in many instances, the mechanization service itself. Finally, there was no other technological resource that demanded such large-scale cultivation and could serve as a lever of the reorganization of peasant holdings. The tractor was the technology choice of the state, despite the economic costs, because it was such a powerful and immediate instrument of the extension of state power and the redefinition of the social relations of production.

International assistance agencies worked to interject technical advice and evaluation into the environment of Tanzanian development, but for not entirely dissimilar reasons, they were no more successful than Tanzania in keeping the lid on technical excess. In pursuit of broad goals and large constituencies, these agencies serviced the development needs of many countries simultaneously. They defined their technical mandates in terms of specific international institutional goals, rather than in respect to specific national circumstances. They were incapable of tailoring technical and economic advice to suit the immediate context of Tanzanian development. The World Bank recommended a highly capitalized infrastructure to promote transformation agriculture, because that was its approach at that time to Third World development as a whole. Similarly, the ITDG and the ILO recommended small-scale technology because their programs in the late sixties embraced such an emphasis. The FAO sang its song of large-scale mechanization because that was what it had been singing for years. These agencies were unable to redefine the nature of their programs to fit the special, and rather diverse, needs of the country.

So, in the case of aid, there were no complex technological aid packages put together, no programs that addressed the diversity of circumstances. Agencies did not cooperate with each other because of their very different institutional approaches, despite the fact that they were all fighting serious resource constraints. The only reason the ITDG and the ILO cooperated was because of the personal diplomacy of Schumacher. In retrospect, the ILO was totally dissatisfied with the venture, and did not plan any others. There was no interagency dialogue on Tanzanian mechanization, no follow-up, and hardly any acknowledgment of the common problems each confronted. Thus, there were no aid programs in which both small-scale and large-scale technology were supported. And, in fact, agencies were prone to overidentify with the political period in which they operated, and to criticize, as a consequence, the work of those who came earlier or later in the throes of Tanzanian state building.

There was a lack of technical vision on both the national and the international level. The state's suspicion of progressive farmers and its desire to move quickly on its policy of villagization made it uncomfortable with its own technical experts. The people who sat in the Tanzanian Ministry of Agriculture were very often the sons and daughters of the Sukuma, the Chagga, and other tribes that had profited from colonialism and formed the core of the country's cash croppers. These technical experts could not endorse the plans of the party to send thousands of tractors into regions in which they would ultimately lie idle and rust, and so they were not consulted. The international assistance agency's suspicion of the work of other agencies and its desire to be able to operate in many countries at once, regardless of circumstance, made it uncomfortable with technical recommendations that went beyond the bounds of its own institutional ideology. Other agencies were potential competitors for the interest of both Third World clients and industrial contributors. Cooperation and the pooling of resources and knowledge raised the possibility of losing one's own institutional character, as did the orientation of programs to national circumstances rather than international constituencies. The blame for the technology failure can be equally shared.

Kenya's state building and the focus of its economic development as a whole was essentially elitist in character. The politics of agricultural mechanization in Kenya were politics of narrow constituencies, limited state administrative expansion, and a landed elite which controlled agricultural production. This necessarily resulted in income inequities and ethnic chauvanism, but it also resulted in technology transfer efforts which cost the state relatively little in an administrative respect, while earning it relatively more in respect to technical success. When the tractor was introduced into peasant cultivation, it was frequently coopted by the large-scale farming sector. This was unjust socially and politically, but technically it meant that the costs of the program as a whole were minimized. When the tractor was extended to ethnic groups on the peripheries of state power, it was then redirected to the provinces and districts in which the Kikuyu dominated. Again, this was a policy with which the state created political insiders and outsiders, and the technology was, as a consequence, relocated to regions where the infrastructure of technical support was greater. Thus, Kenya pursued a technology transfer program in respect to the tractor that was socially unjust, technologically safe, and administratively and economically inexpensive. There were no tractor deserts in Kenya, but rather a high concentration of resources in those regions of the country that were deemed economically and politically most important.

While the constituency Kenya hoped to reach with agricultural technology was more narrow than that pursued by the state in Tanzania, the tractor, in Kenya, was nevertheless perceived to be the same kind of tool of state building. Whether capitalist or socialist, states are interested in using the technology to set down a technical grid upon which the social relations of production will be based. These relations of production were, in important respects, very different in Kenya than they were in Tanzania. Kenya worked to create a landed elite, a wealthy class of farmers who received from the state the economic resources and policy supports necessary for prosperity. In contrast, Tanzania attempted to collectivize agriculture and organize peasants into cooperative modes of operation. The structure of rural property ownership and income was, as a consequence, more egalitarian in Tanzania than it was in Kenya. The political utility of large-scale holdings, and thus of the tractor, was, despite this, very similar in both countries. Both sought to aggregate land ownership and find a large-scale economic basis for the centralization of state power. Neither state could survive on rural social relations that were highly disaggregated and in which economic authority was highly decentralized. For both countries, tractors were the means to find a rural social basis for central-ized power. The fate of small-scale technology remains relatively bleak for this reason.

The role of international aid in Kenyan agricultural mechanization was different from that in Tanzania in particulars, but strikingly similar in essential characteristics. Kenya became the target of the change in ideol-ogy that swept through the assistance community in the late sixties and early seventies. Suddenly, the approach to development that it had adopted at independence was considered illegitimate and inappropriate. But in both national contexts, international agencies were more attuned to how their projects met the strictures of their organizational ideologies and goals than to how they were or were not integrated into the processes of national development. For example, the World Bank did not acknowledge the extent to which its own development ideology in the 1960s was in considerable agreement with that of Kenya, nor did it take responsibility for the kinds of advice it had offered at the time. Rather, the organization analyzed ten years of Kenyan economic change as if it had just arrived on the earth, an interplanetary observer with no responsibility for Kenya's first choices or its current economic circumstances. Its ideology had changed, and so, as far as it was concerned, must Kenya's. Never mind the implications of the past. Further, this degree of self-focus meant that while all agencies were aware of the other's interest in Kenyan agricultural mechanization, none moved to begin a formal policy of cooperation or follow-up. In fact, some of what was done was redundant and a waste of assistance resources. The projects themselves were well conceived; the experts well informed and sensitive to the environments in which they operated; the agencies in tune with the lessons of the past. However, none of this was enough to make for really effective assistance. A cooperative research effort in the area of small-scale technology, a cooperative as-sessment of the economy or the THS, a cooperative follow-up on aid to the western regions of the country would have more quickly and more effectively advanced the prospects of technology transfer.

Thus, neither Kenya nor Tanzania was able to benefit from an interna-tional assistance effort of technical consensus and cooperation. In this respect, assistance in the area of agricultural mechanization was quite different from that in seed improvement. At the same time, Kenya was more successful than Tanzania in its effort to introduce new mechanization resources, because it narrowed its constituency, limited its goals of social transformation, and pursued a relatively small-scale program of institutional extension and agricultural mechanization. Despite the disarray on the international level, Kenya had some successes. And, while Kenya also experienced some technological failure, it was not on the same scale as that experienced by Tanzania. Tanzania's broad-scale goals of equity overlapped with the universalism of international assistance, resulting in a disastrous technology transfer program. Finding a constituency for successful technology transfer was an extremely difficult proposition given the relationship between resources and goals on both the international and national levels. Both countries were, however, able to use the tractor as a political instrument for the extension of state power and the redefinition of the social relations of production. In this respect, all that the international agencies can do, regardless of the degree of technical consensus, is to watch. Those characteristics that make the technology so difficult to successfully introduce to small peasant farmers also make it a very powerful representative of state power in the countryside.

CHAPTER 4

THE GREEN REVOLUTION REGIME: TECHNOLOGICAL PARADIGMS AND INTERNATIONAL COOPERATION

T WO DECADES AGO Third World agriculture was presented with a technology of revolutionary capabilities. New varieties of basic food crops were developed, which as a consequence of genetic research and the alteration of basic plant structure were better able to exploit the resources of the physical environment and produce more food. In Mexico wheat yields increased from 11.5 bushels to 40 bushels an acre. In India the average farmer, who once reaped 800 kilos of wheat, now produced 1,300.[1] In Asia as a whole the value of the rice harvest increased by $300 million.[2] Countries thought to be losing the race between population growth and agricultural production capability had become self-sufficient in food production. The Green Revolution had arrived. The international investment in Third World agricultural research, first initiated by the Rockefeller Foundation in Mexico in 1943, had paid off handsomely. And the success of these research efforts was, perhaps, even more stunningly significant for the international assistance community than the production figures themselves might have indicated. At the time that it became widely acknowledged internationally the assistance community was becoming aware of, and assessing, the extensiveness of failure in so many other areas of Third World economic development. The Green Revolution stood out like an economic oasis in a desert of policy despair.

The discussion among development assistance agencies on the significance of the new technology gave birth to an international assistance institution of an entirely novel orientation. Founded upon a technological success of considerable magnitude, with no bureaucracy to speak of and a narrow constituency, and relying extensively upon outside, independent technical advice as a basis for decision making and program growth, the

Consultative Group on International Agricultural Research (CGIAR) was created to further and expand the work that the Rockefeller Foundation had begun. It pooled the economic resources of most major assistance organizations—both bilateral and multilateral—to produce new technology specifically suited to the economic and physical circumstances of Third World countries. It seemed able to elevate itself above the ideological controversies that embraced so many assistance organizations, imbuing the good for which it was responsible with a kind of neutrality which allowed for widespread international support.

How and why was this possible? How was it that states avoided in one technology area the duplication of effort, diffused resources, fragmented institutional capabilities, ideological debate, and competitive approach that so characterized the other? In this chapter, an answer to this question will be developed. There is no doubt that the organization of assistance in the area of improved food crops is very different than that in the area of agricultural mechanization. The diversity of economic, organizational, and ecological circumstances in the Third World became the basis for technical innovation rather than political confrontation.

The Founding of an Assistance Regime

Most international development assistance agencies were created on the heels of a global war. The technical mandates that they embraced were to be carried out in the name of grander visions of international peace and justice. The Consultative Group on International Agricultural Research (CGIAR) has many of the same general technical interests of other members of the international assistance community but few claims on the larger arena of world politics. Its special contribution to world order is almost entirely technological. The single-mindedness of its technical purpose is firmly rooted in the circumstances that resulted in its founding.

The Rockefeller Foundation pioneered the idea that direct investment in agricultural research for Third World environments was an important contribution to Third World development. The program it began in Mexico in the 1940s was as new to the foundation at that time as it would be to the assistance community some thirty years later. The foundation had done no prior work in agricultural research. It did, however, have extensive experience in the funding of science. Until the sixties, when its work in agriculture would become predominant, the foundation was engaged largely in medical research and education, public health, and the control of endemic diseases.[3] Internationally, it supported the work of the League of Nations in these areas, and in the halcyon years of that international organization expected to turn over its medical programs to the League. But, increasingly impressed with the administrative red tape and political battles that characterized the League's social and technical programs, the Rockefeller Foundation decided to continue its own private funding of international medical research and public health programs.[4] Its work in the areas of malaria and yellow fever and its contributions to the development of medical education in the United States ultimately earned it international acclaim. The institutional sensitivity it developed to the special requirements of scientific research—narrow technical goals and purposes, long-term financial commitment, and avoidance of political controversy—were made a part of the food technology regime that it helped to establish.

Research breakthroughs in the United States and Asia in the 1920s set out the basic perimeters of the technical innovation that supported their own agricultural modernization and that would lead to radically increased food production for Third World countries decades later.[5] The Mexico program, funded by the Rockefeller Foundation in 1943, was based upon that research tradition, and thus the success of the program was not entirely a surprise to those responsible for it. Certainly, the impact on Mexico was less of a surprise than the impact upon the foundation itself. New varieties of both wheat and maize were developed, spurring sharp increases in Mexican food production by the 1950s. Further, the Mexican technical infrastructure was enhanced through the training of indigenous scientists. By the 1960s there were approximately thirty doctorates in the agricultural sciences in a country where there had previously been none.[6] For the Rockefeller Foundation the consequences were perhaps even more far-reaching. Members of the Mexico team formed a leadership cadre which produced a new direction in foundation policy and expanded the commitments of the institution to international agricultural research. By 1960 an early member of the team was made foundation president, and the agricultural sciences had overtaken medicine as a primary area of investment.[7] With the support of another major American foundation, the Ford Foundation, the national project in Mexico was turned into an international institution, the International Maize and Wheat Improvement Center (CIMMYT), and several more were created—the International Rice Research Institute (IRRI), the International Institute of Tropical Agriculture (IITA), and the International Center of Tropical Agriculture (CIAT).

In the fall of 1970 and the winter of 1971 a series of meetings were held in Bellagio, Italy to explore the idea of a broad international effort to support the work of the centers. At the conclusion of these meetings a new international agency had been established which two dozen assistance actors would ultimately join. There were two primary circumstances that led to the internationalization of the work of these two private foundations. First, the collective support that was mobilized at Bellagio came about as a consequence of the financial considerations of both the foundations and the other assistance agencies. Despite the Ford Foundation's active involvement during the sixties, it had become increasingly difficult for the financial needs of international research to be met by the budgets of two private foundations. Just to maintain the centers that the Ford and Rockefeller foundations had established, much less to expand into other food crop areas, more extensive financial support was needed. At the same time, bilateral and multilateral agencies were involved in their own critical reassessment of program commitments. Assistance budgets were under attack in industrialized societies impatient with the lack of dramatic and widespread change in the Third World. Investing in Green Revolution technology was a way to renew confidence and direction without radically increasing overall assistance commitments. Second, the decision to form a new aid actor was very much a consequence of the power of the new technology. The accomplishments of the Green Revolution in Asia and Latin America in the 1960s and the certainty of the Rockefeller and Ford foundations about the research tradition that they supported had raised high the expectation of assistance agencies that perhaps a technical fix had indeed been found for the problem of Third World economic development. The level of interest in the work of the international research centers was great and had already led some assistance agencies to invest in international research institutions and to cooperate with Ford and Rockefeller foundation scientists on food projects in specific Third World countries. The technology itself sold bilateral and multilateral aid actors on the wisdom of the creation of a new assistance actor.

Ideology and Institutional Structure

As is the case for other assistance agencies, the institutional structure and politics of the CGIAR are governed by an organizational ideology. The difference is that its ideology has been developed around the capabilities of a technology, not vice versa. The constituency to which the CGIAR addresses itself is extremely narrow in a political respect and strongly rooted in the technical community that assesses its work. Thus, the way decisions are made, the budgetary process, and the administrative apparatus are extremely responsive to the needs of research and technical development.

The agricultural assistance approach prior to the Green Revolution was one that assumed that the technology that could improve production already existed.[8] The policy focus that followed from this assumption resulted in assistance programs in the areas of agricultural extension and community development. Assistance attempted to revamp delivery systems without taking cognizance of the good that they were delivering; it was an alteration of structure without changing content. The lesson of the Green Revolution was that it was not the delivery systems or the surrounding institutional environment that was important but rather the development of a technology that could exploit to the best advantage the inputs coming from both the economic and physical environments. According to the CGIAR, it was now well understood how to develop this technology, and in the future successful agricultural development would simply be a matter of making a commitment to the necessary agricultural research. As two Green Revolutionaries explain:

> The strictly technical aspects of agricultural improvement are reasonably well understood by a small number of scientists. Given the availability of individuals fully qualified to understand and attack the problem of production through the scientific method, it is possible in almost any nation to bring about improvements of real significance.

Admittedly, the task is formidable, but it can be done just as surely as engineers can build a superhighway across a nation or space scientists can place a satellite in orbit.[9]

The ideology of the CGIAR was quite simply an exhortation to heed the lessons of the Green Revolution and promote improvements in Third World food crops. It identifies technology as a carrier of the most positive attributes of scientific research into Third World countries and peasant cultures. Changes in social and economic institutions that earlier assistance programs attempted to effect are much more rapidly produced by the introduction of new technology. It was the technology itself, not the fancy assistance package in which it might come, that would dramatically transform the economic capabilities of Third World countries and overcome the problem of Third World food production.

This organizational commitment to technology as the answer to the most fundamental of Third World economic development problems is the pivot around which the structure of the CGIAR swings. Decision making within the group is not guided by a constitution or any formal statement of institutional norms or rules, but rather it is determined by technical principles. No formal votes are ever taken. Decisions on policy programming are set once a consensus is reached among member states, and this consensus is informed by the work of two advisory bodies, the Technical Advisory Committee (TAC) and the International Food Policy Research Institute (IFPRI).

The Technical Advisory Committee is the group's vehicle for the review of the work of the research centers, and as such is the more important source of policy advice. The TAC is a committee of scientific consultants who serve for two years, are drawn from a variety of disciplines including economics, and are recruited equally from industrialized and nonindustrialized countries. This is a committee of outsiders whose own disciplinary or national commitments are balanced by those of other members. A very small secretariat in Rome at the FAO administers the TAC, organizes its visits to the centers, publishes its reports, and when necessary represents its interests within the group. On the basis of in-depth evaluations of the work of the centers, the TAC makes policy recommendations to the group concerning the quality and overall direction of research. In other words, it states its preference on what work should be funded and what should not, which programs should be continued and which should be terminated. In the most fundamental sense, it charts the policy direction and assistance investments of the group.

The International Food Policy Research Institute also advises the CGIAR on research funding. Established by the group in part as an early-warning system for food crises, it determines the significant global trends in food production, national research capabilities, population growth, and technical manpower in Third World countries. Where were the big gaps in production? Who were the most important food importers? Where was the population increasing at the most rapid rate? Thus, while not directly concerned with the work of the centers, IFPRI's analysis of global developments in the Third World were also intended to help determine where money should be spent. The TAC is probably more important in respect to short-term decision making—which centers should be given the most support, which projects the most attention—while the analysis sponsored by IFPRI provides a basis for longer-term considerations in respect to the establishment of new programs or the redefinition of older ones.

Though scientists and technical experts essentially make its policy and are, as well, among the most important constituents to which the work of the group is addressed, it is the states and international assistance agencies that keep the organization afloat financially. The budgetary process of the CGIAR is extremely flexible. There are no formal quotas or equations for the assessment of budgetary contributions. The character of this arrangement was from the beginning a very attractive feature of the group's structure for member states.[10] Following the reports of the TAC upon the research progress of the various international centers, members decide to which centers they will provide support. A very small financial secretariat in Washington, housed at the World Bank, lobbies for centers whose budgets have not been voluntarily supported by enough donor countries to maintain their established research schedule. The centers themselves have considerable autonomy within the CGIAR and can appeal to donor states and agencies directly. If the director general or the board of trustees of an individual center are interested in a program of research that the TAC does not recommend, they can lobby for the importance of their own programs and receive support independently of annual group funding.[11] The group provides for 85 percent of the funding of the centers. The other

15 percent is provided outside the formal structure of the group and is allocated as a consequence of the fund-raising activities of individual centers. Thus the assumption is that the research accomplishments must sell themselves.

Underlying this freedom to choose is a requirement that member states and institutions be capable of making a long-term commitment to overall support. In fact, the most important criterion of group membership is the financial capability to invest in the work of the centers over the long haul. Research, according to the group, and in the tradition set for it by the Rockefeller Foundation, can only take place in an institutional context of continued support. It is not a short-term enterprise. It is to be expected that some programs will be terminated due to lack of support, but in the main members must expect to sustain the work of the international research network as a whole. Between 1972 and 1976, six members—the Rockefeller Foundation, the Ford Foundation, the World Bank, the Inter-American Development Bank, the United States, and Canada—each contributed over $10 million to the group's work.[12] Other member states and organizations whose financial support was sustaining, though not as substantial, include Australia, Belgium, Denmark, France, the FAO, Germany, Japan, the Kellogg Foundation, the Netherlands, New Zealand, Norway, Sweden, Switzerland, the United Kingdom, the United Nations Development Program, and several regional banks. There are no developing countries who are members. Thus, its membership and its immediate national constituency is quite a bit more narrow, and in fact, more elitist, than that of most assistance organizations.

The budget as a whole gradually increased throughout the seventies to support an expanding research capability. A year after its founding the group spent $23 million on agricultural research. In 1973, again, the group allocated $23 million to the work of the centers. In 1974 the budget grew to $34 million, and in 1975 to $45 million. By 1977 the CGIAR had a working budget of $79 million.[13] In that year it was decided that the work of the group would be consolidated, and the expansion in research centers that characterized these years would not be continued. This decision was not taken in an atmosphere of intense political conflict or in a context of program failure, or for any other reason than that of financial caution. At that point the group was composed of eight research centers—the International Maize and Wheat Improvement Center (CIMMYT) in Mexico, the International Rice Research Institute (IRRI) in the Philippines, the International Institute of Tropical Agriculture (IITA) in Nigeria, the International Potato Center (CIP) in Peru, the International Crops Research Institute for the Semi-Arid Tropics (ICRISAT) in India, the International Center for Agricultural Research in Dry Areas (ICARDA) in Lebanon, the International Laboratory for Research on Animal Diseases (ILRAD) in Kenya, and the International Livestock Center for Africa (ILCA) in Ethiopia—one regional association, the West African Rice Development Association (WARDA), and one central gene bank, the International Board for Plant Genetic Resources (IBPGR). Research work was being carried out in cereals—rice, wheat, maize, sorghum, millet; roots—manioc and cassava; pulses, legumes, and tubers—pigeon peas, chickpeas, cowpeas, yams, and potatoes; and livestock. Cereals remained the single most important part of group research, because they continued to be the major source of calories in Third World diets, and were the crops for which major research breakthroughs had been most successful.

While the budget of the CGIAR would continue to grow—by 1983 operating costs had expanded to $164.7 million—the basic research infrastructure was established by the mid-seventies.[14] The CGIAR was almost entirely devoted to the production of new technology, and its governing politics almost entirely defined by the technical requirements of that production process. A multitude of states and agencies had come together to globalize the isolated successes of the Green Revolution and in the process created a structure of cooperation with few ideological battles, a highly focused pattern of resource investment, and an assistance capability with almost no bureaucracy but great technical expertise. Certainly, it was the case that states had somehow chosen to construct this unusual assistance effort, had chosen to form an organization that would address a very narrow technical and political constituency, and had chosen to sacrifice larger world order concerns. However, the opportunity to make such a choice was offered by a technical success grounded in remarkable technical consensus on the creation of a new technology. That technical consensus, or paradigm, formed the basis for powerful political cooperation.

International Regimes and Technological Paradigms

The postwar institutionalization of world order has given way to a period of transition in which multilateral relations have moved out of, and in some respects beyond, the bounds of the international organizations in which they were orginally enclosed. As the policy problems states confront challenge the founding mandates upon which international institutions were based, new avenues for the facilitation of multilateral relations have been sought. In the process of this change the importance of the underlying normative agreements that inform international institutions has been revealed. It has become more and more apparent that the rules that govern international cooperation are, in many cases, more important than the structure that monitors those rules. As a consequence, for the student of international organization, the concept of regime has begun to replace that of organization or system as the centerpiece of analysis.

International regimes are, according to John Ruggie, "sets of mutual expectations, generally agreed-to rules, regulations or plans," which determine the actions of states in respect to each other in areas of policy in which they share a common interest.[15] International regimes are founded for a variety of purposes and in response to a variety of circumstances. In the study of international cooperation scholars have identified trade regimes, money regimes, human-rights regimes, security regimes, and the like. A regime, whatever its substantive focus, might embrace several organizations, organizations and states, states and private actors, or any number and kind of international political actors. It is also possible for several regimes to be contained within one organization. Whatever the policy orientation or the number of actors, the essence of a regime is the existence of a consensus that supports the maintenance of mutual expectations, rules, or norms. This consensus might grow out of any number of different ideological or bargaining contexts. In the case of the regime that the CGIAR oversees, it is the existence of a technological paradigm that is the basis of highly consensual decision making and effective interstate and interagency cooperation.

Scientific paradigms are, according to Thomas Kuhn, "universally recognized scientific achievements that for a time provide model problems and solutions to a community of practitioners."[16] Paradigms orient the work within a tradition of inquiry to one set of questions rather than others and provide the methods with which to determine right and wrong answers. The development of technology is, as is the case with science, characterized by the rise and fall of paradigms that define the perimeters of acceptable research. But technological paradigms, in contrast to scientific paradigms, are in part defined by the human environment in which technology works. While science is concerned ultimately with truth, technology is concerned with solving the practical problems with which individual societies struggle. The importance of model problems and solutions—"exemplars," as Kuhn also calls them—are established by questions raised by society and answers that have social, economic, and political as well as technological implications.

The technological breakthroughs that led to the diffusion of higher-yielding rice and wheat further diffused as well the technological exemplar that had first fostered agricultural development in the United States and Japan and later in parts of the Third World. That exemplar became the model upon which the CGIAR was based. The question with which the development assistance community was concerned was the omnipresent development question, "How do we develop the Third World?" This was not, in the first instance, a technological question, but with the introduction of "miracle seeds" into the farming systems of several Third World countries, the assistance community entered into the business of adopting a technology paradigm as an answer to it.

At the center of the new assistance effort and the pardigm were the following rules. Research was to be: 1) addressed to increasing productivity; 2) defined by the production problems of individual crops, thus embracing a commodity orientation to research; 3) based upon genetic manipulation—the alteration of the basic structure of the plant through the identification of traits that result in higher yields; 4) further refined in relationship to the different requirements of major ecological zones; and 5) based upon multidisciplinary teams of scientists who make a career commitment to Third World food research and the paradigm.

In cereals, breeding for greater productivity has meant breeding for basic structural change in the plant—shorter, thicker plants that make better use of the sun's energy, absorb more fertilizer, allow for denser stands, are insensitive to day length, and produce more grains in a shorter growing season. The creation of a germ plasm bank for each crop is the basis upon which this breeding takes place. In many cases, the systematic collection of material, most importantly from the center of origin of the crop, was an entirely new development not rivaled by any similar national or international collection. Literally thousands of varieties are collected, screened, and then crossed in order to develop plants that yield higher amounts of food. Multidisciplinary teams of scientists—plant breeders, geneticists, soil scientists, agronomists, entomologists, pathologists, and agricultural economists—work together in a common effort to develop new plants which are able to take better advantage of the inputs from both the natural and the human environment. Systematic testing of different varieties for different ecological zones is an important part of the research effort as well. Material developed at one international research center is sent to others and to national institutions at different elevations within different rainfall and temperature regimes. Besides providing material for their own breeding and testing, the centers make contact with the international scientific community in the Third World in order to duplicate the norms of their own community and transfer the paradigm. They assist with library and documentation services, train national staff, and host seminars and conferences.

The force of this paradigm and the exemplar of Green Revolution technology established the rules of operation for the CGIAR as well as for the research program. The success of the research institutes and the growing contact between the institutes and the food programs of aid agencies led to the founding of the regime. With its founding a regime ideology was formalized that gave expression to the technical self-confidence of the researchers. Institutional capabilities were developed which, like the ideology, were primarily technical in nature and designed to facilitate the efficiency and excellence of the process of technology development. The CGIAR provided minimal institutional services. It concretized a set of norms that were technical in nature and built its own organizational mode of operation around those norms. That which held the research community together held the regime together. And when one was challenged, so was the other.

The Paradigm Challenged: Whither the Regime?

The breakdown of a scientific paradigm is preceded by "the persistent failure of the puzzles of normal science to come out as they should."[17] So it is with technological paradigms. The puzzle of the Green Revolution that has not entirely come out as it should is the puzzle of adoption. In the early seventies J. George Harrar, a scientist who was with the Rockefeller Foundation team in Mexico, when interviewed concerning the diffusion of Green Revolution technology, stated: "I feel very frustrated. It's said that if you build a better mousetrap the world will beat a path to your doorstep. We built a better mousetrap but people didn't come."[18] While the ability of the new varieties of rice and wheat to double and triple production was unquestioned, the extent to which they were being integrated into Third World farming systems was more problematic. In 1972–73, several years after the initial success of the Green Revolution, only 35 percent of the wheat and 20 percent of the rice grown in Asia were high-yielding varieties.[19] This problem has been addressed by the research centers in a variety of ways. The research agenda of some has been altered to include research that is tailored to previously ignored aspects of Third World farming systems. Other centers have begun to take an active role in the strengthening of national research capabilities. International assistance agencies and states that are especially concerned with the problem of more widespread adoption have acted to support the new work of the centers. In each of these cases—the definition of a research agenda and the development of national capabilities—it is the paradigm that is being challenged.

The question of a research agenda has been raised by those who see the technology as carrying a inherent bias, putting it in the hands of rural elites and impeding its diffusion to the average peasant cultivator. Both scholars and international assistance researchers have determined that the technology is capable of making rich farmers richer and poor farmers poorer.[20] The technology was developed primarily to maximize production. The new crops were, as a consequence, highly dependent on other technological inputs. For example, plants were bred that were able to absorb more fertilizer, more efficiently, and thus could produce more food. However, for the farmer's yields to approximate those of the international centers, he was, in many cases, expected to use not only fertilizer, but pesticides, irrigation, and mechanization. The expense of this package of technologies is often beyond the limits of the farmer's yearly income. Breeding for greater productivity has not excluded breeding for disease and pest resistance, but with the reconsideration of research objectives that took place after the full impact of the Green Revolution had been evaluated, the CIAT, IRRI, CIMMYT, and IITA began to develop seeds that were less dependent on fertilizer than earlier varieties and made pest and disease resistance a research priority.[21] At the same time, IFPRI advised the CGIAR to focus research on rain-fed agriculture, because there was a serious and basic lack of good water control and irrigation in most Third World countries.[22] In other words, crops were to be improved with the assumption that these ancillary technologies would not be available to the farmers who adopted the new seeds.

A second issue pertaining to research design, raised soon after the success of the initial technology, concerned the fact that semi-arid, arid, and hot tropical environments had been excluded from the center's research. Breeding for harsh and marginal environments became the special mandate of new centers like ICRISAT. As in the case of breeding for pest and disease resistance, breeding for conditions of drought, high temperatures, and other extreme environmental conditions became a potential competitor with productivity as the primary goal of research. It was not that productivity was displaced as the most important aim, but that its status was being slowly eroded as breeding took on the responsibility of diffusion.

As these alterations in the work of the research centers were made, it became more and more apparent that the initial assumptions about Third World farming upon which genetic research was based were replicated in only small parts of the Third World. An interest in better understanding the character of the problems faced by Third World farmers and the economic constraints within which they operated grew and fostered center involvement in the sponsorship of farming systems research. This was not a matter of adding another discrete goal to the research agenda but of entirely redefining the process of doing research. Farming systems research is the study of the ecological and economic characteristics that determine the conditions within which a farmer works. A farming system includes soil, plant life, animal life, and climate as well as the availability of credit, the level of income, the existence of transport, the structure of markets, and other economic considerations. Farming systems research directly questions the centrality of commodity orientation. Most Third World peasant farmers are not monocroppers; they grow high-yielding varieties along with other food and cash crops. They frequently practice integrated pest control, and in general, intercropping is widely practiced. The need to investigate two crops simultaneously, or to study how one crop grows in relationship to another, is fundamental to Third World farming systems research. Furthermore, such research places considerable emphasis on economic investigation in relationship to the hard sciences, implicitly questioning the role played by the crop breeder. At the very least, it complicates the problem of planning for structural change in a plant when the functional task at hand is no longer limited to one major economic goal—productivity—and a simplified physical environment. Its promise is that it can greatly increase the likelihood that the technology developed is something in which the Third World farmer is interested. The IITA was actually founded with a special mandate in this area, but for a variety of reasons the program has had difficulty getting off the ground.[23] Despite this, farming systems research has been added to the work of CIMMYT, IRRI, and ICRISAT. As a proportion of the budget of individual centers, it constitutes 37 percent of the IITA's budget, 21 percent of IRRI's, and 18.5 percent of ICRISAT's.[24]

The paradigm has been challenged in yet another way as well. In many ways, this challenge—the need to develop national diffusion capabilities—presented the CGIAR with more difficulty than the issue of research design. Farming systems research may in the future present international agricultural research with a new paradigm around which research for the Third World is organized, but for the time being, it is still second in importance to commodity-oriented research. On the other hand, the decision on the part of some states, agencies, and centers to begin the task of institution building in the Third World put the CGIAR in the business of taking responsibility for a whole new task. Technology development and technology diffusion were, it was clearly recognized, two totally different activities. Technology diffusion would begin to involve the CGIAR in more traditional development assistance activities, and it threatened to make the group even more directly aware of the imperfections of the paradigm as a guide to its work.

As now understood, all activities that involve the diffusion of research—even in terms of the testing of and experimentation with material originally developed at an international center—are considered to be part of the center's "outreach" program. Outreach, the responsibility that international centers have for the diffusion of the technology they develop, is an issue that has gradually become extremely controversial among the centers and within the CGIAR. Some see outreach as being as important as the group's work in technology development itself. Others are concerned that center staff in such outreach programs overreach their capabilities and endanger research developments that are ultimately of greater significance. The CGIAR's own Review Committee concluded, in 1976, that:

> a number of factors can potentially distort the balance and integration of components of the program. One of these is cooperation with national programs (formerly known as outreach). Although this cooperation is a vital component of the research mandate of all centers, the demand on the centers to help strengthen national programs through the developing world greatly exceeds the capacity of the system to respond. Extensive involvement can distract a center from its primary research mission and place an undue burden on center management.[25]

CIMMYT, the center responsible for the development of maize technology, and the one in most direct contact with East Africa, has been one of the leaders among the international centers in pushing for greater commitment to outreach. While IRRI is the acknowledged leader in fostering successful research collaboration among national research institutes—its Asian research network has resulted in joint research planning and common research enterprises among rice-growing states—CIMMYT has been actively involved in building national research programs and advising on extension and diffusion.[26] In 1974 its board of trustees urged CIMMYT to establish a more extensive and better-staffed program to support the development of national research programs. Members of the CGIAR who have found themselves in sympathy with this effort and who have themselves provided financial support for CIMMYT's outreach include the World Bank, the Ford and Rockefeller foundations, and the USAID.[27] The Ford Foundation is, in particular, strongly committed to the notion that while the Green Revolution has been a technical success, it has not been an institutional success.[28] For agricultural development to continue beyond its initial goals, there must be national institutions across the globe that can continue to test, modify, and adjust the technology to local conditions.

CIMMYT's outreach includes an international network embracing eighty countries which tests the technology CIMMYT develops and which sponsors training, conferences, and publications. More importantly, unlike some other centers, CIMMYT runs national programs of research and diffusion, sees economic research and economic policy advice and evaluation as a central part of its mandate, and meets with national policymakers regularly on variety of topics having to do with agricultural development.[29] Having provided assistance in the establishment of research and technology diffusion programs in several Third World countries—Lebanon, Turkey, Egypt, Nepal, and Tanzania—CIMMYT is now in the business of establishing regional offices. These efforts have largely been supported outside of the core budget, but were nevertheless reviewed by the TAC, which suggested that regional offshoots of CIMMYT's work might best accomplish the goal of diffusion.[30] The first such regional unit has been established in Central America, and others are in the process of being established in the Caribbean, Andean, Southeast Asian, and East African regions. Two senior scientists will be posted in each region and will serve as liaisons between the countries of the region and CIMMYT. They will supervise testing, advise governments, and carry out research work in one or more countries in the region in conjunction with that country's individual research and diffusion program.

CIMMYT's work in this area, and the interest of donor states and agencies in extending it, led to the creation of the International Service for National Agricultural Research (ISNAR) in 1979. According to the task group that set down its mandate, "at the root of the problem in most countries is the need to plan, organize, and manage research more effectively."[31] The establishment of ISNAR is an explicit acknowledgment by the CGIAR that something must be done about outreach beyond the work carried out by individual centers. It is also an attempt to take some of the burden off of center staff with the development of a new institutional capability. ISNAR is not intended to duplicate the work of the centers, but to work with individual countries in the identification of their research needs and the ways they might work with the group in the formulation of their own research policy and in the determination of how external finance might be found to support the creation of adequate research facilities.[32] This service is modeled on a private organization which was established in 1975 by several leaders in Green Revolution technology and policy for whom research policy, planning, and organization on the national level were as important as the development of an international capability and who, instead of waiting for the CGIAR to act, set up a private nonprofit corporation to address these issues.[33]

In the early years of Green Revolution technology development, the diffusion of research and the implementation of extension were thought to follow from the imperatives of the technology itself. The CGIAR was founded upon the assumption that a good technology could substitute for the lack of infrastructure, institutional development, and economic services in Third World countries. As the group began to extend the work of the centers first established by the Rockefeller and Ford foundations, the full force of the critique of the Green Revolution began to be digested by both scientists and policymakers associated with the new technology. One of the conclusions drawn by those who took the critique seriously was that it may have been a mistake to underrate the importance of the circumstances to which the technology was addressed. The resulting challenge to the paradigm has not given us a new paradigm. Rather, individual rules have been questioned as anomalies are discovered, and the absence of explicit rules for diffusion has been criticized. In Kuhn's terms, normal research has been expanded.

But the implications of this dialogue are important to the nature of an assistance regime like the CGIAR. Much of its success has been predicated on the belief that the activities normally undertaken by an assistance agency could be, in this case, foregone. The consensus that led to the founding of the regime was based on the notion that a new technology could right many of the assistance wrongs of the past. It was also, implicitly, based on the idea that the members of the CGIAR themselves possessed the institutional capabilities to move the technology out of the centers and into farmers' fields. The regime can survive the addition of new types of research strategies. It cannot survive the establishment of competitive institutional capabilities. If the CGIAR begins to carry out its own extension projects alongside of those of the FAO, the World Bank, and USAID, it will begin to play the kind of political game that characterizes assistance in general. If, on the other hand, member agencies and states are able to concur on how to jointly assist individual Third World countries in the establishment of national research and extension capabilities, then the norms that govern the regime will have been formalized in another area of collective policy. The precedent for this kind of cooperation has already been set, as we will see in the coming chapter.

CHAPTER **5**

EAST AFRICAN MAIZE
AND THE COMPARATIVE POLITICS
OF TECHNOLOGY SUCCESS

KENYA AND TANZANIA inherited research institutions biased in the direction of cash crops, but while Kenya rose like a phoenix from the colonial structure of research, Tanzania sank like a stone. In fundamentals, Kenya and Tanzania played the same political development game. Both states approached agricultural research as a way to expand the authority and legitimacy of the state, but as was the case in the implementation of agricultural mechanization projects, the values that determined the stakes for which the game was played led to very different outcomes. Tanzania pursued a technically and economically more ambitious program in an effort to reach the majority of peasant farmers. Kenya was satisfied to target particular regions and ethnic groups as primary recipients of the new technology. The result was that high-yielding varieties of maize ultimately revolutionized Kenyan agriculture, while Tanzania was left highly dependent on regional and global food imports.

The efficiency and capability of the assistance that was offered might have offset these distinctions in state building. The Green Revolution regime of international research institutes and associated assistance agencies carried out impressive programs of research and extension, moving the technology very quickly out of the technician's lab into the farmer's field. However, there were sharp discrepancies in preindependence social and economic change which were the basis for an important distinction in the initial level of interest of the international actors and in the ability of the states themselves to identify the significance of such technological assistance. The technical legacies were the same—cash crop research—but the patterns of constituency development and resource investment pursued by the colonial state in Kenya opened a door through which the Rockefeller Foundation and the resources it had to offer could easily enter. In contrast, such patterns made it much more difficult in Tanzania for the state or the international agencies which aided it to find an appropriate point of entry.

Finally, the character of the technology introduced pushed the Kenyan economic successes even further than the state wished to see them go, while powerfully blocking the most basic goals of the Tanzanian effort. In this chapter I will examine in what respects a colonial legacy of development gave Kenya a head start in the development of food production; why high-yielding varieties of maize proved to be slippery instruments of class politics; how the state, nevertheless, attempted to use them to such ends; and why an international structure of aid that is highly cooperative fosters more effective development assistance projects.

Colonial Legacies

Britain is said by some to have acquired its colonial empire in a fit of absent-mindedness, and by others to have carefully orchestrated its imperialism in response to important geopolitical and economic interests. Whatever the causes of the British occupation of so many Third World territories, actual patterns of colonial development varied greatly.

There was no grand imperial plan for the economic or political exploitation of Tanganyika. The imperatives that galvanized such a policy in some other African colonies were missing. There were no fabulous mineral riches to be extracted, no European civilization to be protected, no rich agricultural trade to be coopted. As a consequence, economic and political penetration proceeded haphazardly, following no particular design. At times, programs were established that reflected narrow, or momentarily mobilized, external economic interests. In other periods, the state attempted to address the economic needs of the native population. It never made a strong commitment to either an external or internal constituency. A pattern of political development emerged that embraced this conflict, and technical development followed behind. In contrast, in Kenya there was coherence and constancy in the patterns of both eco-

nomic and political development. This was largely the case because the
constituency to which the state addressed itself was clearly and unambi-
guously defined. The settler community and its economic and political
interests were at the center of the economic and political development of
the colony. The course of economic development set down by this strategy
of colonial state building was decidedly different than that established in
Tanganyika, because it was clearly linked to the systematic development
of a specific portion of Kenya's agricultural sector. As a consequence,
while during colonialism Kenya did not acquire any greater technical
resources, its postindependence technical development programs were
founded upon a more coherent economic focus and the necessary systems
of technical support were in place.

Britain began to settle Kenya at the turn of the century. The European
settlers who came to Kenya, like so many other immigrant populations in
other parts of the world, transferred their own social order and values
from the mother country to their new homeland. In the case of Kenya, one
of the most significant transferrals was the introduction of a European
cereal culture. There was considerable experimentation by early settlers to
determine what crops might be grown, but the pastoral ideal that they
brought with them from Europe emphasized wheat, maize, and cattle.[1] As
Lord Delamere, one of the earliest and most important leaders of the
settler community, once noted, "I started to grow wheat in East Africa to
prove that though I lived on the equator I was not in any equatorial
country."[2] Wheat ran into immediate and serious problems with rust (a
tropical plant disease) and with the cost of production. Settlers continued
to grow it, and the state actively supported its cultivation, because of the
kind of commitments Delamere identified, and because it was the basis of
the settlers' own subsistence. Maize had traveled to East Africa via the
Portuguese soon after its introduction to Europe in the fifteenth century.
However, it was not extensively cultivated until the arrival of European
settlers. According to Hinga and Heyer:

> Maize was one of the early pioneer crops because it required little
> skill and little capital, it gave a quick return, and it provided a ration
> for labor on the farm. For these same reasons, it was regarded as an
> eminently suitable crop on which to base the expansion of mixed
> farming in the highlands.[3]

As a consequence of its extensive cultivation by white settlers, maize eventually replaced sorghum and millet, crops more resistant to drought, as the dominant food crop in both Kenya and Tanzania. Tanzania began to import maize from Kenya during the colonial period.

This cereal culture entailed extensive state support of European settlers. European settlers were protected from competition from the external market with the establishment of high import duties on all externally produced cereals and with the regulation of internal prices for both producers and consumers.[4] When the depression hit, agricultural credit, direct subsidies, and the remission of railway and administrative charges were granted. World War II created food shortages within the empire, and farmers were encouraged and supported by the government to expand the acreage devoted to grains. At the conclusion of the war, the Increased Protection of Crops Ordinance, which provided short-term credit, the Guaranteed Minimum Return (GMR), and the market protection established under earlier policies were all made permanent fixtures of the structure of support provided to European settlers. R. S. Odingo believes that, in general, it was the protected market that was the most important foundation upon which cereal cultivation was expanded both before and after the war.[5]

Despite the extensiveness of these supports, in Kenya, as in Tanganyika, there were no massive investments in agricultural research in the area of food crops. Both countries were part of a regional structure of research which emphasized cash cropping. Coffee research was carried out at Lyamugu in Tanganyika and at Ruiru in Kenya; sisal research at Mlingano in Tanganyika and at Thika in Kenya; pyrethrum research at Ol Joro Orok and Molo in Kenya; and tea research at private plantations throughout the settler colony.[6] And, in Tanganyika there was extensive and highly successful cotton research. In both colonies, some attention was given to maize research with the arrival of tropical corn rust in West Africa.[7] While the fear this crop disease induced was far greater than the impact the disease would actually have in East Africa, research was initiated to develop resistance to rust, leaf blight, and other plant diseases in both Kenya and Tanzania.[8] These programs remained relatively modest until East Africa became part of the efforts of the Rockefeller Foundation and CIMMYT to improve local maize varieties. Thus, there were no

TABLE 5.I.   Use of Cultivated Area in Kenya, 1920–1960
(1000 hectares)

Crop	1920	1930	1938	1960
Maize	128.0	808.4	456.0	574.7
Wheat	19.0	287.1	231.7	1,004.0
Barley	2.4	11.3	17.0	126.7
Oats	2.0	12.2	16.6	113.4
Total cereals	851.4	1,119.0	721.3	1,818.8
Coffee	112.6	388.8	396.1	288.3
Sisal	117.5	437.4	488.8	703.1
Tea	—	33.6	55.1	149.9
Wattle	47.0	45.8	79.8	345.5
Other plantation crops	8.9	12.6	6.1	1.6
Total plantation crops	286.0	918.2	1,026.9	1,488.4
Pyrethrum	—	—	27.5	160.8
Fruit and vegetables	8.9	11.3	20.3	62.4
Fodder crops	2.4	4.5	17.8	139.3
Other crops	105.3	42.9	46.6	394.1
Fallow	108.5	308.6	298.5	473.0
Grass leys	—	—	—	87.1
Total cultivated land	662.5	2,404.5	2,157.9	4,623.9

SOURCE: R. S. Odingo, *The Kenya Highlands: Land Use and Agricultural Development* (Nairobi: East African Publishing House, 1971), p. 56.

significant distinctions between the two countries in terms of internal research capabilities.

At independence, the European mixed cereal farming sector in Kenya was said to be one of the most productive sectors of the economy. It certainly supported the majority of European settlers. By the 1930s maize and wheat accounted for 48.9 percent of all cultivated land; sisal and coffee for 31.4 percent.[9] At independence, there were 2,500 mixed farms, 390 ranches, and 590 plantations.[10] But despite this, cash crops were the most important sources of colonial revenue. Following World War I and up until World War II, sisal and coffee were the strongest parts of the colonial economy. By 1960, just prior to independence, coffee and sisal had been joined by tea and pyrethrum as the major cash crops and made up among themselves 75 percent of the total value of agricultural exports. In other words, there was no comparative advantage to the cultivation of wheat and maize in Kenya, and they did not earn significant revenue for the colony. The earliest wheat farmers got nine bushels an acre, while in Australia farmers produced eleven bushels and in America, fourteen.[11] The case of maize was not much different, and the productivity of the cereal sector as a whole did not improve dramatically with time.

Thus, there was an economic price to pay for cereal development. In the 1950s European settlers made a strong argument for the fact that they were the economic foundation of the colony. They were the source of foodstuffs for the regional market as a whole, while African producers remained at subsistence level. But the reason they were in such a position of production preeminence had little to do with their greater productivity and much to do with the state's subsidization of their enterprise. In the last decade of colonial rule, European cereal farmers received double the price for their crops that they would have received on the world market. According to William O. Jones, the task of feeding Kenya would have been done more efficiently through the purchase of African surplus and international imports.[12] The state's economic support of the settlers reflected a constituency choice, and while that choice may not have been economically rational from the standpoint of the costs of support and the productivity of the average European farm, it resulted in the creation of the modern infrastructure and institutions upon which the new state could build. It is into this kind of a support system that agricultural technology is most readily transferred.

International Assistance and National Research

A decade after independence, Kenya had strengthened its research capabilities in food crop research and developed high-yielding varieties of maize especially suited to Kenyan farming systems. In the same ten years, Tanzanian agricultural research slowly deteriorated, and its dependence upon Kenya's accomplishments grew. The interest of the international assistance community in Kenyan agriculture made a considerable difference in the resources that were made available to each state, as did the state's own ability to identify the importance of the new technology.

The Rockefeller Foundation first expressed its interest in the sciences in East Africa in the late fifties. As independence approached, the foundation, along with most United Nations assistance agencies and bilateral aid programs, sent policy advice and evaluation missions to African countries to consider in which ways it was most appropriate to contribute to economic development. In the case of East Africa, members and former members of the Mexico program participated in the assessment of the needs of the region. It was as a consequence of an early mission that one Kenyan scientist was sent to Mexico and Colombia to visit two international centers concerned with maize research. In 1958, Michael Harrison, a Kenyan maize breeder, returned from his trip with breeding material that would form the basis of Kenyan research breakthroughs in the sixties. The Rockefeller Foundation subsequently sent four Kenyans, all Europeans, to Latin America in order to spur Kenya's work in wheat and maize with its own technological research.[13] It would provide consistent support for maize and wheat research at Kitale, a maize research center in the White Highlands which until the middle-fifties was concerned with grasses, and at Njoro, the wheat research station founded by Lord Delamere.

The center of origin breeding material that Harrison brought back to Kenya, Ecuador 573, became the parent for the improved maize that Harrison and his coworkers developed at Kitale. The Latin American variety was crossed with Kenya Flat White—the local maize which was the result of decades of intercrossing African maize with the variety brought to East Africa by immigrants from South Africa at the turn of the century. With the incorporation of new material, the genetic base was broadened. Ecuador 573 was chosen by Rockefeller Foundation scientists because it was well suited to the physical environment of Kenyan farmers.[14] The result, Kitale Synthetic II, was released to farmers in 1961. Kitale Synthetic II was 30 to 80 percent superior to local varieties. On the heels of Harrison's success with composites, the United States funded more Kenyan maize research as a part of its East African Major Cereals Project. U.S. assistance built upon the research at Kitale but redirected it to the development of hybrids. Three American crop breeders were sequentially posted to Kitale, from 1963 through the late seventies, to support continued research and development. The first of a series of hybrids was released in 1964. Subsequent varieties, which yielded much more than Harrison's composite and with greater dependability, were released throughout the sixties and seventies.

Both the composite and the hybrid research program shared a common orientation to productivity as the most important research goal, were based upon the expansion of the genetic base of research, were led by multidisciplinary teams of scientists that worked for basic structural change in the plant, and were geared to the environmental characteristics of the largest maize-growing region, the White Highlands. At the same time, USAID scientists took the Kitale program in a new direction. CIMMYT's maize research, unlike the research done by other international centers in the areas of wheat and rice, was oriented to the development of composites or synthetics, rather than hybrids. USAID, in contrast, was most concerned with hybrids, and less interested in synthetics. Both are high-yielding varieties (HYVs), but for the farmer, there are two major differences between the composite and the hybrid. The first produces less per acre than the second, but the seed for each new crop of composite maize can be taken from the harvest of the last. In the case of hybrids, seed must be grown on seed farms, and the farmer must then purchase new seed for each crop.

USAID's decision to assist agricultural research in Kenya was a part of a long but not particularly distinguished history of U.S. involvement in Third World agricultural research and technology transfer. In 1969, USAID began to fund research at CIMMYT, and just prior to the founding of the CGIAR, it made contributions to IRRI, IITA, and CIAT. In the early seventies, it began to fund national food crop research programs in many countries and even more closely bound its own assistance to that of the regime as a whole.[15] The Kenyan project was a harbinger of the kind of work it would do a decade later. The cooperation between the Rockefeller Foundation and USAID, the way in which one research project built on the work of the other, would characterize a multitude of food projects in the 1970s.

The research breakthroughs that were a consequence of the joint Rockefeller Foundation/USAID work put Kenya far ahead of Tanzania—and many other African countries for that matter—whose agricultural research in the first decade of independence continued to follow the cash crop agenda laid down by colonial authority.[16] The most significant achievement of the Tanzanian maize research program in these years was the development of a composite, which produced 25 percent higher yields than the local variety at medium altitude. A U.S. Department of Agriculture assessment of Tanzanian agriculture in the sixties found, not surprisingly, that national maize research was making little progress and that hybrid seed from Kenya was being imported by European farmers. It predicted that Tanzania was likely to remain an important customer of American grain in the coming years.[17] And, in fact, by the late sixties, Kenya became an exporter of cereal grains, while Tanzania began to import food both from Kenya and other grain-producing countries (see figure 5.1).

Why was Kenya able to profit from the developments that were occurring in the international research regime, while Tanzania was not? There are many reasons for this difference in postindependence research development. To begin with, while the Rockefeller Foundation transferred material from Mexico, Colombia, and Kenya to maize-breeding programs in Tanzania at Tengeru, Ukiriguru, and Ilonga, there was no concerted effort to provide the necessary technical leadership. No direct contacts were established between maize breeders in Tanzania and those at CIMMYT. No other scientists were sent to Tanzanian breeding stations by the Rockefeller Foundation or other bilateral or multilateral aid agencies. The assistance effort was simply less well conceived in respect to technical leadership.

In Kenya the state confronted at independence a mobilized constituency with a strong interest in agricultural research and the development of local high-yielding plant varieties. Tanzania had no such constituency working to influence the state and direct its international aid. Rhodesia had released maize HYVs for commercial production following World War II. Kenyan European farmers hoped to benefit from the same technological improvements enjoyed by other European communities in Africa. The Africans who joined them as members of the large-scale farming community were equally eager to influence the state to invest in technological development that would be of direct benefit to their economic pursuits. In Tanzania there simply was no equivalent group of farmers. The settler community was too small to exercise such influence, and large-scale

Figure 5.1.   Balance Between Imports and Exports of all Grains in East Africa, 1955–1975 (1000s of metric tons)

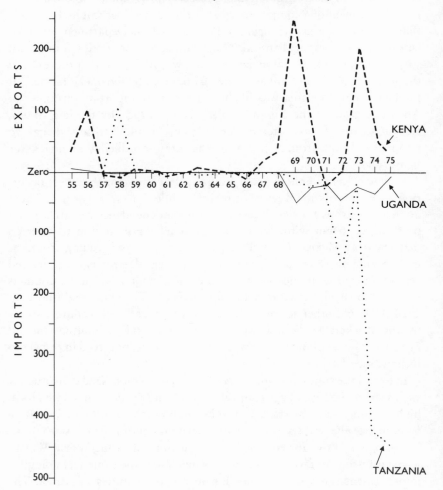

SOURCE: Philip W. Porter, *Food and Development in the Semi-Arid Zone of East Africa*, Foreign and Comparative Studies/African Series 32 (Syracuse, N.Y.: Maxwell School of Citizenship and Public Affairs, Syracuse University), 1979.

farming was concerned with plantation rather than food crops. There was no African class that inherited the tradition of large-scale farming of cereals. And, in fact, the state was completely uninterested in the establishment of such a class. Peasant agriculture and the subsistence cultivation of food crops did not seem reason enough to sponsor an ambitious food crop research program.

Finally, national agricultural research capabilities were, in general, not identified by the Tanzanian state as an important component of its overall development strategy. Tanzania confronted more serious manpower shortages within its research structure as a whole at independence than did Kenya and did less to remedy the situation. The legacy of the colonial past was aggravated by a government impatient with long-term development investments. In 1963, the year in which the Rockefeller Foundation introduced new material into the Tanzanian maize program, the government's annual assessment of agriculture noted that "fears expressed last year on the possibility of premature retirements among senior officers have been realized."[18]

Most plant breeders continued to be Empire Cotton Growing Corporation scientists, and manpower shortages were not limited to breeders but were widespread. Research expenditures during the early sixties were a very small proportion of overall development expenditures, and thus did not arrest the flight of expatriate technical expertise.[19] During the Second Five Year Plan the manpower problem was made worse by a government policy that resulted in the transfer of staff from station to station and from crop to crop with little regard for the training or the specialization of the individuals involved. Resident expatriate scientists left at an even greater rate, because they felt that the Ministry of Agriculture did not understand their needs.[20] The lack of manpower, an adequate research budget, and a secure work environment undermined the organization of agricultural research throughout the country. In the late sixties, an expatriate Tanzanian crop breeder candidly evaluated the situation in the following manner:

It would be dishonest to ignore the hard fact that with the single exception of the cotton varieties produced at Ukiriguru none of the new varieties produced in Tanzania in other crops have had any major impact upon farming in Tanzania.[21]

By the end of the first decade of development the Rockefeller Foundation attempted to catalyze a more ambitious regional program in order to support research breakthroughs that might reach Tanzanian farmers. The foundation hoped to rectify the situation in Tanzania with an invigorated program of technology transfer between the two countries, and believed that the prospects for greater regional cooperation were good. In 1970 the head of the East African Agriculture and Forestry Research Organization (EAAFRO), the East African regional research organization that was an inheritance from British colonialism, formally proposed that the members of EAAFRO establish a regional cereal and legume institute. The justification given by EAAFRO and supported by the Rockefeller Foundation concerned the conservation of resources and the effective diffusion of research accomplishments. The member states were, however, most interested in the establishment of national capability. Kenya wanted to project its own research program and ensure "that the Kenya National program should not be weakened or diluted to serve the regional needs of other countries."[22] Tanzania was even more intent on breaking its dependence on Kenya and strengthening its own national capabilities. According to the Rockefeller Foundation's report:

> It was emphasized strongly that Tanzania must assure the adequacy of its internal programs to serve Tanzania. . . . Tanzania must be sure that her internal needs are adequately cared for in the event that future development would make the access to technology, genetic materials, seed stocks, etc., needed by Tanzania less readily available from neighboring countries than is the case at present.[23]

Regionalism was rejected, first, for reasons of national prestige. Both countries wanted national programs run by and for nationals. Secondly, for Tanzania the inequity of the research status quo was a further reflection of the trade imbalance, which had developed between the two countries in food as well as other goods. Tanzania wanted an independent research program in order to have an independent food sector. The importation of material had in the past been followed by the importation of seed. Thirdly, it was increasingly recognized, both internationally and regionally, that Tanzania was not tailoring its agricultural development to its equivalent of the Kenyan White Highlands. The physical environments it wished to reach were at a lower altitude and more arid. As one Rockefeller Foundation official explained, the Tanzanian minister of agriculture "went begging for" varieties that were suited to medium- and low-altitude environments. Further, the economic context in which Tanzania's small-scale holders farmed was very different from that which characterized the food sector in Kenya. Tanzania needed its own research breakthroughs if it were to catch up with Kenya.

Trickle-Down Development and the Diffusion of Agricultural Technology

Upon the heels of research success, the Kenyan government took a number of steps to assist in diffusing the new technology directly into the large-scale cereal sector. The state accepted the colonial claim that this sector was essential to the overall health and development of the economy. This judgment was supported by major international assistance agencies like the World Bank. The Bank offered the following assessment of the sector in its earliest economic survey of the Kenyan economy: "The deliberate replacement of large-scale with small-scale production may mean the destruction of capital assets and the adoption of less efficient forms of production."[24] However, despite the confidence of such agencies as the World Bank and the orientation of the government, it was now widely recognized that the productivity of the large-scale farmer needed to be greatly improved. If the sector as a whole were to continue to be a source of revenue, the yield per acre would have to be increased. At independence the export of maize was generally at a loss to the government treasury. The price guaranteed to the farmer could not be recouped in sales abroad or in East Africa. This was the case despite the fact that local prices for grain and bread were inflated.[25] One Department of Agriculture analyst termed maize, along with wheat, "an embarrassment to export."[26] Large-scale farmers were simply not as productive as their counterparts in other cereal-producing countries: in the late fifties and early sixties, large-scale Kenyan farmers averaged six bags of maize per acre. Through its investment in agricultural research, the government hoped to dismantle the protective price structure, control local price inflation, and compete internationally over the long term with other cereal producers. To assure the accomplishment of these objectives, it developed a program of diffusion that was targeted to the large-scale holder.

The new varieties were almost immediately adopted by large-scale farmers in the Trans Nzoia, Uusin Gishu, and Nakuru districts of the Rift Valley. By 1964 one-half of the large-scale farmers in the Trans Nzoia were using Kenya Synthetic II, and by the end of the decade 90 percent of the corn planted by large-scale farmers throughout Kenya was hybrid.[27] The agricultural credit offered by the government to diffuse the research success of the Rockefeller Foundation and USAID projects was intended to get the technology into the large-scale sector as rapidly as possible. The requirement that a farmer own fifteen acres or more put small farmers out of the potential pool of borrowers for Guaranteed Minimum Return (GMR) crop credit.[28] Fertilizer subsidies were provided by the government on terms that made them available only to large-scale farmers. And within the large-scale cereal sector, there were farms and farmers who were given special consideration. As one provincial report noted, "It has been found difficult to control G.M.R. applications because many personalities take part. It has been observed that some farmers seem to have direct contact with Nairobi without passing proper channels."[29] Credit programs were, in general, carefully monitored and highly centralized. Those farmers that were most important to the state and in many cases the direct inheritors of European farms were the primary target group for the new technology. While not specifically addressed to the sector per se, agricultural extension also gave large-scale farmers in need special treatment.

Government interest in the support of the large-scale farming sector led it to become involved in a grass seed company, the Kenya Seed Company, established in 1957. The company became the primary avenue for the production and distribution of Green Revolution technology. Along with a new research program, credit, extension, and the continuation of a protective price structure, government participation in seed production and distribution came about to ensure the necessary support for large-scale cereal production. The government created a program of supervision for the company's seed farms, which resulted in standards of production equal to those established by the International Crop Improvement Association.[30] The Kenya Seed Company worked closely from the beginning of

TABLE 5.2.   Hybrid Maize Grown in Kenya, 1963–1974 (hectares)

Year	Large-Scale Farms	Small-Scale Farms	Total
1963	158	4	162
1964	11,615	708	12,323
1965	22,137	8,110	30,247
1966	25,860	15,269	41,129
1967	55,501	46,642	102,143
1968	36,501	51,331	87,832
1969	39,500	64,291	103,791
1970	47,110	97,372	144,482
1971	63,785	149,864	213,649
1972	73,944[a]	206,804	280,748
1973	53,370	264,699	318,069
1974	39,214	292,358	331,572
1975[b]	46,742	327,908	374,649

SOURCE: EAAFRO, *Record of Research: Annual Report* (Nairobi: EAAFRO, 1974), p. 94.
[a]Adjusted per Kenya Seed Co.
[b]Estimated.

its interest in maize with the Kitale research station and with the large-scale farming community.[31] Initially, it began the bulking and distribution of seed for large-scale farmers only.

Despite the expectations of government policymakers and national and international researchers and despite the orientation of the government's diffusion policy, the new technology was also rapidly adopted by small-scale holders. As John Gerhart's study demonstrated, the large-scale farmers took the initial risks, but in the high-rainfall, high-altitude areas of the Rift Valley and Western Province (the White Highlands), both small- and large-scale farmers adopted hybrids at a rate that exceeded that in the American Midwest at the peak of the diffusion of new seed.[32] By 1975 there were approximately 46,742 hectares of maize under cultivation in the large-scale farming sector, and 327,908 hectares under cultivation in the small-scale farm sector (see table 5.2). Ninety percent of the total maize crop was being grown on holdings of less than five acres.[33] While there are no comparative statistics on the bag yield per acre, it is known that small-scale farmers produce maize at a much lower cost and a much higher profit than do large-scale farmers. By the late sixties, large-scale farms produced around 120 Ksh per acre of crop planted, and small-scale farms produced 635 Ksh.[34] Thus, the small-scale African peasant not only adopted the new technology but began to dominate in the production of a food crop that had once been the purview of large-scale European farmers. As a consequence of the adoption of the new technology and a number of other comparative advantages, the small-scale producer grew maize more efficiently than the large-scale farmers.

The rapidity with which small-scale farmers adopted the high-yielding varieties took the researchers at Kitale by surprise. As the Kenyan scientist who pioneered the composite program explained:

> It was felt that small scale farmers would not pay the high price needed each year for hybrid seed and too many would plant second generation seed. It was, however, hoped that those who did well with synthetics would later move onto hybrids as their husbandry standards improved. However, the impact of the higher-yielding hybrids was so great that soon after their release, in 1964, it became impossible to sell synthetics to either small-scale or large-scale farmers and improved synthetics are now used only in hybrid combination.[35]

No less surprised were those in government who were responsible for the large-scale farmer focus. No coordinated public programs had been developed to reach the small-scale holder, and a half-hearted effort at agricultural extension had failed. Kenya's agricultural extension set out several thousand one-acre plots demonstrating the higher productivity of the new technology.[36] According to the Select Committee on the Maize Industry, this effort was counterproductive:

> Much of the impact of the research that has been done on different aspects of maize production has been reduced by the inefficient use of extension and other communication channels through which recommendations based on research results are transmitted to farmers. The Committee found widespread dissatisfaction with the Government extension services.[37]

Kenya's Special Rural Development Program (SRDP), which was launched in the early seventies, was designed to attempt to rectify this problem. It was, however, the work of the Food and Agriculture Organization, which focused its fertilizer project on maize production, that turned extension into a highly effective tool for the introduction of new technology to the small-scale holder.

The project that the FAO initiated in Kenya was not immediately welcomed by the new agricultural research establishment. The importance of fertilizer to agricultural development—especially maize—was a point of considerable controversy within the local scientific and technical community. Agronomic research had been funded by the Rockefeller Foundation at Kitale to complement maize breeding. Those working with this effort concluded that next to the actual adoption of HYVs it was the time of planting that was the most important determining factor of production increases.[38] Because of the feeling that improved husbandry was, in general, more important for higher maize yields than was fertilizer, the research station was not certain that there was any value in a project that would attempt to introduce the use of fertilizer to small-scale holders. It urged the FAO project to sell the triple message of seed, improved husbandry, and, only lastly, fertilizer. Surprisingly, the FAO did just this.

The effectiveness of the FAO's own project was, ultimately, quite dependent upon the extent to which it worked in cooperation with both the researchers at Kitale and the government's own extension efforts. The FAO's fertilizer program is very similar in concept and implementation to its agricultural mechanization program. The agency's commitment to technically sophisticated and capital-intensive technology cuts across individual technology choices. Thus, the agency continued to attempt to prove that fertilizer itself was of special value to Kenyan peasant cultivators. During the tenure of the project in the late sixties and early seventies, the FAO assisted Kitale in field trials which indicated that in some areas of the country fertilizers were perhaps of more importance than had been originally appreciated.[39] But the primary impact of the work of the FAO was not in the area of such technical reassessments but rather in the scope and organization of agricultural extension. Because of the FAO's project, the small-scale maize producer was reached with the message of the Kitale research station. Despite the FAO's very different agency mandate, and its competitive instincts in respect to the work done by Rockefeller Foundation and USAID scientists, it followed up on the work of research assistance and provided Kenya with the kind of extension program needed to reach the small farmer.

The FAO carried out 10,331 demonstration plots over a six-year period; 5,240—or, in other words, just over half—were carried out on the high-yielding varieties of maize developed at Kitale. The method used duplicated the agronomic research done by the Rockefeller Foundation scientists, at the same time that it sold the agency's message. A three-part demonstration plot was constructed. The first section was grown with hybrid seed and the recommended husbandry practices, the second with phosphate, and the third with phosphate with a nitrogen top dressing.[40] As importantly, these plots were not located at research stations or extension offices but were placed in the midst of small-holder farms, most often near a well-traveled road in a farmer's field.

Despite the emphasis on fertilizer, the impact of these demonstrations did not always accrue to the benefit of the FAO. In Vihiga District, in Western Province, an area designated for special government assistance as a part of the SRDP, there were 120 demonstration plots laid out each year for four years, 1970–74. There was, however, no increase in the use of fertilizer, and as one evaluator pointed out, the farmers given special SRDP assistance to buy fertilizer used it instead for other farm purchases.[41] However, while the demonstration plots may not have increased fertilizer use, they did increase the utilization of the new maize. According to Heyer, Ireri, and Moris, by the early seventies, maize was the one exception to the rule that extension did not effectively meet the needs of the small-scale farmer.[42] Both the Select Committee on the Maize Industry and Kitale scientists saw the FAO extension effort as a more systematic and careful extension effort than the earlier work of the Ministry of Agriculture.

The FAO fertilizer project in Kenya was in many ways not unlike other fertilizer projects that it had sponsored under the Freedom from Hunger Campaign. It was directed to private holders and the private sector. It reflected the agency's interest in introducing modern technology as a spur to productivity. It assumed that increased productivity was the most important criterion by which to gauge the accomplishments of the project. It brought to bear its own considerable capabilities in mobilizing the resources of multinational corporations. Nevertheless, the work of the project was essentially coopted into that of the international research regime. Unlike the work it sponsored in the area of agricultural mechanization, the FAO did not work at cross-purposes or compete with other agencies. While working to demonstrate the importance of fertilizer, it helped to effect an agricultural revolution in Kenya in the area of food production. There was never any formal international agreement with respect to field assistance. It was the success of the technology itself and the momentum of the research that continued to be carried out at Kitale that oriented the FAO to build on the accomplishments of the Rockefeller Foundation and USAID. When the FAO began its work in the late sixties, it was riding a wave of technology adoption by small-scale holders which had not yet crested. Its own work would expand that segment of the food crop sector that came crashing into the beachhead of the political goals of the state. It was the FAO's orientation to interagency cooperation and follow-up that made all the difference in respect to the successful transfer of the technology and led to the confrontation between small-scale farmers and Kenya's strategy of state building.

The belief that large-scale farms are necessary to the economic strength of agriculture is an assumption about agricultural development that has limited the extent of actual economic transformation in many Third World countries, Kenya included. Large-scale cereal farms in the White Highlands were transferred intact to African large-scale holders and peasant corporations, because it was thought that any alteration in the scale of production would diminish productivity as a whole. In the production of maize in Kenya, this has now proven to be false. Small-scale farmers are capable of making essential technical improvements and, as a consequence, become more efficient producers. In the late sixties, following the widespread adoption of the new technology by both large- and small-scale holders, the government introduced a new pricing policy in respect to maize. Hoping to capitalize on the impact of the new technology, the government lowered maize prices and attempted to reach export parity (see table 5.3). As a consequence, large-scale farmers took thousands of acres of maize out of cultivation. Small-scale farmers remained unaffected and, in fact, in response to the growing availability of the new technology and the effectiveness of agricultural extension, increased the amount of HYV maize in production.

While the wrong constituency was benefiting from the transformation, the hopes of the Ministry of Agriculture with respect to research and maize were being realized. The fact that it was the wrong constituency that benefited made, however, a great deal of difference to the state. The

TABLE 5.3.   Guaranteed Producer Prices: Maize in Kenya, 1962–1972 (Ksh)

Year	Price Per Bag
1962	24/
1963	27/
1964	28/50; 32/50; 29/50
1965	32/50; 34/
1966	37/
1967	29/50
1968	28/
1969	25/
1970	25/; 30/
1971	35/
1972	35/

SOURCE: Republic of Kenya, *Report of the Select Committee on the Maize Industry* (Nairobi, 1973), p. 13.

large-scale farmers were in trouble and called upon the government for assistance. These large-scale farmers formed an extremely important group of government ministers, politicians, civil servants, and other elites. Their economic problems were many. They were being pushed out of the production of a major food crop. They had no experience in other agricultural pursuits. And they were in debt to the government, which had taken loans from major bilateral and multilateral aid agencies to purchase European farms after colonialism. The government had, thus, a number of reasons for bailing them out and promptly did so. In the early seventies, the pricing policy of the Ministry of Agriculture was reversed. Colin Leys believes that large-scale farmers not only effectively lobbied the government for a change in policy, but that it was the president himself who made the final decision to raise producer prices.[43] The price per bag continued to rise in the seventies, and in 1975 the government increased the price by a whopping 30 percent, from 50 Ksh per bag to 65 Ksh per bag.[44]

With these pricing policies, the government in one stroke maintained an extremely important constituency, affirmed its preferred rural social relations of production, and undermined its own economic self-reliance and that of its agricultural sector. The development and diffusion of the new technology was an unqualified success. Many more farmers than anyone had anticipated were reached as a consequence of effective and coordinated international research and extension assistance. It was clearly not the scale of production that limited the diffusion of the technology. However, in a political respect, the technology was too successful. The state was not displeased to reach small-scale holders in the high-potential regions of the country; some of them were Kikuyu. But it was genuinely threatened by the transfer of economic power that the technology's successful diffusion seemed to portend. While unable to reverse the integration of the new technology into peasant agriculture, the state was able to manipulate macroeconomic policy in order to shape the economic, social, and political effects of the technical change.

Reaching the Periphery: Technological Bias and National Capability

In 1970 Tanzania invited USAID to evaluate its program of agricultural research and make recommendations for the future. As the establishment of ujamaa villages was placed at the center of the pursuit of socialism, the creation of a strong economic foundation for rural transformation grew in importance. The increase in political support for ujamaa was, however, only one of the factors that led the state to reconsider its past neglect of agricultural research. Kenya was in the throes of a veritable agricultural revolution, and comparisons between the two countries were inevitable. Kenya was becoming a stronger regional, and potentially a strong international, exporter of food at the same time that Tanzania's dependence on food imports was growing. The fact that its neighbor to the north was able to feed its own population helped to catalyze Tanzania's interest in agricultural research.

The USAID policy advice and evaluation team confirmed that research in Tanzania was in considerable disarray.[45] One-half of all positions were vacant. Many staff members were only temporarily assigned to a particular research unit or program. There was a pervasive lack of proper supervision and almost no coordination among researchers engaged in similar projects. The mission called upon the government to institute a reform of the organization of research through the establishment of a National Agricultural Research Center. This new government bureaucracy would organize the diverse work done within Tanzania and determine research priorities. As importantly, the mission concluded that for such a reorganization to work, the country would need to import external scientific expertise to fill vacant positions and establish the necessary technical leadership.

Tanzania was not pleased with USAID's analysis. It challenged the international agency's concern with training and education by stating outright that USAID did not understand that "a person well suited to research would be valuable within one year of his first degree."[46] It was also critical of the suggestions of the agency with regard to internal policy reform. Tanzania believed that what was most necessary was to link into the work of the international centers. USAID's interest in assisting Tanzania weathered this disagreement. A national project was designed and funded at $2.5 million. It was to include four components—maize breeding and agronomic research, food legumes agronomy, soybean research, and research planning and administration. The project was to be executed by an as yet unnamed American university. Before American resources were mobilized, Tanzania insisted that the Ford Foundation be consulted on the potential role of international centers in the execution of the project. While Tanzania had been hesitant to involve itself in the Rockefeller Foundation's regional research effort, it was not hesitant to integrate its own new research effort into the work of the international regime.

The project did not change in essentials with the addition of the Ford Foundation but it was incorporated into the regime and as a consequence reflected its biases. Ford was in complete agreement with USAID on the question of research organization. The government ultimately replaced its director of research with a new individual who was less idiosyncratic in general research policy and more committed to food crop research. The government was urged, as well, to implement other aspects of the original policy advice and evaluation mission's recommendations. At the same time the overall research direction of the project was given greater focus. Soybeans were dropped and local food crops, especially maize, were given immediate priority. The Ford Foundation asked CIMMYT and IITA to be responsible for the implementation and evaluation of the project. The Ford Foundation was very concerned about the development of local capability and the overhaul of national policy—it believed that the work of the centers was "directly related to the capacity of national research programs to absorb, adapt, and utilize this research."[47] But the development of national capacity must meet certain technical criteria. The foundation saw the articulation of a technical methodology for the implementation of the research as something that the centers would impose upon the nation. Ultimately, the resurrection of an individual research station, as undertaken by scientists associated with the regime, was the model that the Ford Foundation hoped would transform Tanzanian agricultural research as a whole.[48] Or, in other words, Tanzania would adopt the research paradigm upon which the regime was based, and as a consequence its problems of research planning, coordination, and policy would be solved.

While the way efforts were coordinated among international agencies providing research assistance in Tanzania was quite similar to what had taken place in Kenya, the substance of the project's research was distinctively different. The goals of the Tanzanian research program grew out of the interactions among the international agencies involved, but ultimately, the priorities of the government and those of CIMMYT determined the outcome of this interaction. And the priorities of the two actors emphasized the research goals advocated by the international challengers of the regime's paradigm.

The Ford Foundation was interested in breeding for the highest productivity and the highest protein content possible. The importance of productivity was at the center of the CGIAR's paradigm, and the ability to increase protein content as well as productivity was the technical wave of the future. CIMMYT's program of research had traditionally been concerned with composite development. In Kenya it had been responsible for the early research breakthroughs, but it did not sponsor the development of hybrids. Further, it was less interested in the development of high-lysine maize—maize with greater protein content—than it was in the development of farming systems research. CIMMYT was on the cutting edge of the challenges that were being made within the international agricultural research community. In 1974, six months after the arrival of the first project scientists, a national research conference was held, the first in a series of annual conferences. The Ministry of Agriculture presented a working paper on maize research, which argued that the problem of malnutrition in Tanzania was the result of crop failures, not low productivity or protein content.[49] It wanted the project to address the production problems of the majority of Tanzanian peasants, who farmed in medium-to low-potential regions that were plagued by soil and climate problems. The government argued for an approach emphasizing the fragility of the ecology, the vulnerability of harvests, and the nature of traditional farming practices. The MOA asked the project to breed for: 1) drought tolerance; 2) disease and insect resistance; 3) good storage—hard grain that would withstand animal and pest attack; 4) reasonable yields without fertilizer; 5) intercropping with other food crops—millet, sorghum, legumes, groundnuts, and sweet potatoes; 6) reusable seed—in other words composites, not hybrids; and 7) processing under existing practices and technologies.

The importance of the factors emphasized by the government and CIMMYT could not have been better dramatized for the new researchers if Mother Nature herself had arrived in the labs at Ilonga. In the first year of the project, Tanzania was in the grip of a second year of drought. The change in climate seemed to dramatize the points made by the government about the necessity of breeding for drought resistance. The country was forced to import food at unprecedented levels. International assistance was necessary to prevent the food crisis from becoming a famine. However, the drought was aggravated by the intensification of the program of villagization. Peasants resisting the state's program of rural reorganization did not plant, or simply burned crops. Many of these farmers were successful cash as well as food crop producers living in the high-potential regions of the country where drought was not as frequent a visitor. The state had chosen a political direction that would make it more dependent for national food production on those regions of the country embracing the most vulnerable ecologies. Tanzania might have developed regions of the country that were very similar to Kenya's White Highlands, but to transfer new technology to such farmers was to transfer greater economic power to a class of farmers that the state was attempting to marginalize politically. Tanzania wished to reach the majority of peasants, those who were among Tanzania's rural poor and who were in greater agreement, in many cases, with the state's socialist direction. And this meant a research program geared to farmers in low-productivity environments, who often had little experience with the market.

The first project personnel arrived in Tanzania in late 1973. Three years after the USAID policy advice and evaluation mission, a maize breeder and a maize agronomist began work in Ilonga, the designated model research station. The work was under the supervision of CIMMYT and IITA. The director of CIMMYT had made several consultant visits during the previous year. Five trainees had been sent to Mexico by the Ford Foundation in anticipation of the project. While not nearly as successful as the work of Kitale, a new composite was developed in the first three years of the project. Tuxpeno (ICT) gave slightly better yields than other Tanzanian composites and was more resistant to rust.[50] The plant stalk was short and stiff like other Green Revolution varieties but like other Ilonga composites well suited for low elevation and low rainfall. Research was also undertaken on the intercropping of maize and legumes, and in several cases productivity increased as much as 50 percent as a consequence.[51] By the end of the first three years, it was also determined that fertilizer was not economical in low-altitude maize-growing regions.[52] Thus, the work of the project was focused upon increasing productivity but was as well highly attuned to the constraints faced by peasant farmers cultivating crops in underendowed environmental circumstances.

The government was impatient with the new product to generate results. Soon after the first scientists set up shop at Illonga, the project was asked to carry out village trials. Criticized for not reaching the village, the project began to carry out trials in different ecological zones to test the relationship of seed to fertilizer, pesticides, and improved practices in farmers' fields.[53] In 1976 it was asked to carry out from 100 to 200 such trials in ujamaa villages, after which Nyerere called for an extension of these trials to every village. Disregarding the need for careful control and supervision, the Ilonga research station was made responsible for 600 such trials in 1977. The government was interested in making the research project directly accountable for the way in which their research findings did or did not increase the food production of the Tanzanian farmer. While this is not an entirely unusual role for a research station to play, the scope of the village trial program, the manpower constraints of the project, and the fact that the research project itself had just begun to produce results made such a move somewhat premature. However, the government's policy was in keeping with its extremely ambitious and, in many instances, technologically careless approach to agricultural development. Ujamaa was in full swing, and the new village structure needed technical supports if peasants were to accept the policy of rural reorganization.

In fact, the government had begun its own extension program coincident with the initiation of the research project. The National Maize Program was carried out in nine regions of the country—Iringa, Ruvuma, Arusha, Kilimanjaro, Dodoma, Mbeya, Morogoro, Mtwara, Lindi, and Mara—during the 1973–74 and 1974–75 cropping seasons. There was no new research to offer farmers and no material on recommended practices for the major maize regions of the country. It was set up in response to the food crisis and, like tractorization, as a part of the effort to induce peasants into villages. Fertilizer and seed were distributed free of charge, and fertilizer use in maize production went up from 13,000 tons in 1973 to 25,000 tons in 1974.[54] But still the country faced a food deficit. In a highly unusual move, Nyerere contacted the World Bank directly and asked for assistance in the area of food production.

The World Bank sent a policy advice and evaluation mission to assess the scope of the problem. The mission proposed that the country begin with a strong concentration on the development of the country's most important food crop, maize. While cognizant of the constraints that characterized Tanzanian agriculture—lack of data and trained extension personnel, weak supply and marketing systems—the Bank believed that the introduction of simple innovations and techniques would result in the doubling of maize yields. Following the improvements in this most vital area of food production, the Bank planned to assist the country in technical innovation in other crop areas as well. With a focus on the need to transform peasant agriculture, a concern with the introduction of new technologies and techniques, a mandate to make proposals for the agricultural sector as a whole, and high optimism about the ease with which this might be accomplished, there was a striking déjà vu quality to the Bank's plan. The distinctive difference was the fact that its extension program—the new transformation agriculture—would be based upon agricultural research undertaken by Green Revolution scientists. The Bank was now an enthusiastic member of the CGIAR and a true believer in the power of the new technology.

The National Maize Project—a $180 million loan—was initiated by the World Bank in 1975. The Bank insisted, during the loan negotiation process, that the country direct its attention to the high-potential regions of the country—Iringa, Ruvuma, Mbeya, and Morogoro. It criticized the ujamaa program as too concerned with equity, to the detriment of growth. It urged Tanzania to deemphasize villagization, because the effort had resulted in an investment in social services rather than directly productive activities. However, the project as initiated by the Bank included thirteen regions of high, low, and medium potential. It was carried out in the midst of a policy of the forceful mobilization of peasants into new villages, and was organized around the new village structure. In other words, the project as implemented was almost a complete reversal of the recommendations of the Bank's own policy advice and evaluation: 950 villages were to be reached with maize seed, fertilizer, insecticides, and herbicides.[55] The project was a very carefully designed program of integrated agricultural development, which attempted to take into account the diversity of circumstances into which the new technology would be introduced. It embraced the strengthening of extension efforts, the improvement of marketing and supply, and the construction of the necessary infrastructure. It included specific recommendations on the types of technical packages to be introduced depending upon existing husbandry practices.

After the first cropping season, it was apparent that many villages had not been reached by the extension effort. According to Louise Fortman, "extension contact was so scarce" that in one village "the farmers thought the interviewer was the Bwana Shamba."[56] Cooperatives, which were the primary avenues for the distribution of inputs, were disbanded in the midst of the project, making the delivery of project material almost impossible. Farmers in many areas were unfamiliar with the credit arrangements because the previous national program had distributed goods free to villages. The World Bank provided them at only at 75 percent subsidy and expected some degree of payment. Thus, even though the technical and institutional infrastructure was accentuated by the Bank's investment, it was not enough to overcome the gaps in such structures of support.

In 1977 all international actors had made increased commitments to Tanzania in the area of agricultural development. Sorghum and millet were made part of the research program—both traditional food crops, which had been displaced by maize, were better suited to the Tanzanian ecology. The Ford Foundation added an agricultural economist to the project and supported a program of agricultural economics at Dar es

Salaam. The Canadian International Development Research Center (IDRC) began a project at the University of Morogoro to support the Department of Agriculture in its work on intercropping. The country became one of the first two recipients of loans from the UN International Fund for Agricultural Development, the overall emphasis of which was on maize, sorghum, and cassava production. The World Bank, in the second stage of assistance, broadened its extension effort to include other crops and programs. USAID subsidized an increase in the minimum producers' prices and continued to provide food aid.

Despite the extensiveness of international assistance, Tanzania was never able to effect the kind of change that characterized the development of the food sector in Kenya. In fact, it became increasingly dependent upon the international market to feed its people. In 1970 Tanzania imported 431,000 tons of food and received another 148,000 tons in food aid.[57] Between 1974 and 1975, it spent $250 million on food and depleted its foreign-exchange reserves.[58] By the end of the decade it imported, on the average, 108,000 tons a year, despite some improvements in production in the mid-seventies. In 1980, it was forced to spend 20 percent of its export earnings on food.[59] The droughts in the early seventies and the early eighties were an important cause of the increased food imports and aid dependence, but Tanzania's dependence upon external sources of supply preceded the first severe drought and continued despite its absence. Essentially, it was never able to reverse the trend of dependence upon the international market that began in the late sixties. Other African countries, like Nigeria and Zaire, which did not invest in food production and which had large foreign-exchange reserves from mineral and oil production, were also buying sizable amounts of grain on the international market. But no other African country did so on the scale that Tanzania did.

Agricultural Development: Growth, Equity, and Dependence

The story of agricultural research and the development of the food crop sectors in East Africa is a highly paradoxical one. One country, working hard to reach the small-scale holder—farmers who have not directly benefited from the investments of the colonial or the new African

TABLE 5.4. Research Project Budget of Tanzania, 1973–1977

	FY 1973–74	FY 1974–75	FY 1975–76	FY[a] 1976–77	Totals
USAID					
Contract IITA					
Technical assistance	28,000	98,000	143,000	417,000	686,000
Participants			24,000	189,000	213,000
Commodities		65,000	37,000	17,000	119,000
Subtotal	28,000	163,000	204,000	623,000	1,018,000
Direct Expenditure					
Technical assistance	3,000	20,000			
Participants	56,000	10,000			
Commodities	24,000	2,000			
Subtotal	83,000	32,000	157,000	42,000	314,000
FORD FOUNDATION					
Technical assistance	12,725	43,255	30,255	10,654	
Participants	—	14,637	6,131	19,164	
Commodities	18,628	—	2,155	—	
Subtotal	31,353	57,892	38,541	29,818	157,604
TANZANIAN GOVERNMENT[b]					
Recurrent vote[c]			60,241	15,060	75,301
			(500,000)	(125,000)	(625,000)
Development vote[c]	48,795	48,193	64,578	24,096	185,662
	(405,000)	(400,000)	(536,000)	(200,000)	(1,541,000)
Trust fund[c]	3,374	7,742	9,975	10,410	31,500
	(28,000)	(64,260)	(82,792)	(86,400)	(261,452)
	52,169	55,935	134,794	49,566	292,464
Subtotal	(433,000)	(464,260)	(1,118,792)	(411,400)	(2,427,452)
TOTALS	194,522	308,827	534,335	744,384	1,782,068

SOURCE: USAID, *Annual Progress Report, 1976*, Agricultural Research Project, Tanzania.
[a]Budgeted.
[b]Does not include salaries for Tanzanian staff.
[c]Figures in parentheses = Tanzanian shillings.

state—was unable to foster their agricultural development. Another country, working hard to establish a large-scale sector, independent of such farmers, accidentally transferred an extremely valuable technology into the farming systems of small-scale peasant cultivators and triggered a growth in their real productive capability and income. Why should this be the case?

An agricultural revolution eluded Tanzania for many reasons. To begin with, the state simply did not make the commitment to agricultural research that it made to other development efforts. Soon after the initiation of the project, the government cut its budget for agricultural research as a whole by 50 percent. Furthermore, government contributions to the food project dropped precipitously (see table 5.4). While Tanzania was interested in improving its food crop sector, it did not take seriously the necessity of long-term commitment to research. The very important problem of technical leadership—the creation of a manpower capability and the establishment of a governmental commitment to a set of technical goals—was never solved. In the early 1980s there was still only one CGIAR scientist working in Tanzanian agricultural research.[60] One external scientist can not run an ambitious research program. Without government support and focus, the import of the necessary technical leadership simply cannot be effected. One might argue that the cumulative economic problems of the jump in the price of oil, the drop in the price of Tanzanian export products, drought, and the war in Uganda led to such necessary cutbacks. These catastrophic changes in the external and natural environment of Tanzanian development reoriented many traditional development expenditures. But despite these setbacks, the country continued to import large-scale tractors to boost agricultural production. By 1985, there were almost 10,000 tractors in the country, 40 percent of which were inoperable.[61] The country planned to import 109 more with assistance from the FAO. Agricultural mechanization continued to take precedence over agricultural research as a technical instrument of agricultural change.

Secondly, the ecological basis for the research undertaken in Tanzania was not supportive of immediate technological breakthroughs. Because Tanzania was most interested in developing the low- and medium-potential regions of the country—in order to reach poorer peasant cultivators and prevent the growth of rural-income inequities—the development of its food sector was very problematic in a technical respect from the very beginning. The paradigm that governs international research is, in very large measure, attuned to the physical and ecological environments in which the modern Western farmer operates. The work done at Kitale was able to build more easily upon the accomplishments of research in other regions of the world. That done in Ilonga was based upon a more narrow range of potential successes. In this way, it ran right into the puzzle of adoption with which the regime itself struggled. Tanzania needed research for marginally productive ecological environments, a problem the Green Revolution had not yet conquered.

Third, the number of farmers the extension program attempted to reach was similarly too ambitious. In Kenya the primary cause of the adoption of new technology was how well suited the HYVs were to the physical environment in which an individual farmer found himself. But the second and coincident cause was the presence of an infrastructure in the form of markets, transport, extension, and merchants or cooperative societies.[62] Many of the regions of Tanzania that the state hoped to reach with the new technology were on the margins of the national system of goods and services. In attempting to reach beyond the high-potential regions of the country, it was not simply moving into new ecological zones but into areas of relative economic underdevelopment.

Thus, in the case of Tanzania, the technical foundations for change in the production of food crops were not well established and the extension effort was highly diffused. This should not surprise us, given the constituency aims of the state. Tanzania wanted and needed to reach the great majority of peasant cultivators. It embraced a broad constituency and oriented its research and extension efforts accordingly. It was no more political in its approach than was Kenya, but the state-building strategy that it followed undermined the efforts of the international regime and failed to result in significant technical developments. It might have aimed for the development of its high-potential regions, but like Kenya, it did not wish to foster technical success among a group of farmers who were not at the center of its own political development efforts.

In Kenya, the colonial legacy of food sector development coincided with the new state's strategy of political development and as a consequence the same high-potential regions of the country were developed. Upon independence, Kenya inherited from the British a pattern of economic development that focused upon the White Highlands. This pattern was adopted by the new state, because like the colonial state it was interested in reaching a very narrow constituency—large-scale African inheritors of the white farm mantle. But the technology proved to be a very slippery instrument of class politics. It moved across distinctions in scale of production with wild abandon, transferring considerable economic power to small- as well as large-scale producers. There was a broad cumulative impact on the region as a whole of decades of concentrated investment. Small-scale holders had been included in land consolidation, and were a part of a system of transport, communication, and general economic advancement. Small-scale farmers were like large-scale farmers, both psychologically and structurally a part of the national market. Thus, when a technology was developed that placed a premium on ecological, and thus regional, determinants of technological success, there was no way to limit the technology's impact to the large-scale farmer. To develop new varieties of maize for large-scale farmers was to develop new varieties of maize for a particular ecological environment. Because scale of production did not limit the diffusion of the technology—the technology itself was inexpensive and did not have to be used on farms of extensive cultivation in order to be economical—it was adopted by small-scale holders living within the same set of ecological circumstances. The inexpensive nature of the technology, its suitability to the common ecological circumstance, and the integration of the entire region into the national market of goods and services facilitated the development of extremely successful small-scale cereal producers.

Kenya has as a consequence of this strategy marginalized those farmers who grow crops in low- and medium-potential environments. And in regions of the country that are ill suited to the new technology, economic constraints frequently compound physical constraints. In South Nyanza, a Luo region, small-scale merchants who might sell seed, fertilizer, and other agricultural inputs, according to one district report, were "literally non-existent," and there is similarly not always access to a market in which farmers may sell the crops that they product.[63] Thus, the actual adoption of HYVs in South Nyanza was highest in those areas where Special Rural Development Program funds were invested.[64] During the first two decades of research, Kenya seemed unworried by these problems. For the state the fact that such a technical direction might accentuate the problem of production for such areas seemed merely a matter of long-term social justice.

Despite this lack of political concern, the continuation of a national policy of agricultural research will ultimately reach these farmers. It is highly likely that Kenya will develop such regions of the country before Tanzania. This is not a matter of political intent but of the way state building translates into the development of technical capability. There is no question that Kenya has emphasized, and will continue to emphasize, its high-altitude environments. In 1972 Kenya's maize research station at Kitale was staffed with one maize geneticist, three maize breeders and one assistant, three agronomists and one assistant, one soil scientist, one plant physiologist, seven technical assistants, and a number of other staff members. In comparison, at Katumani, a station focused on research for semi-arid and low-altitude environments, there was one maize breeder, an assistant maize agronomist, and four technical assistants.[65] Further, USAID funds work at Kitale emphasizing the protein content of maize with the development of high-lysine varieties.[66] Kenya is not focusing its national strategy on marginal ecological environments, but it has about the same manpower capability in that area as Tanzania. More importantly, it is developing an internal technical elite of much greater scope and capability than that of Tanzania, and thus the work at Katumani is within a national context and community of productive agricultural research. It is also not adverse to the cultivation of a technical elite—its politics are based upon the support of a social elite—and it does not, as a consequence, shy away from a policy of agricultural research expansion. This is further enhanced by increases in external support. By the early eighties Kenya had eight CGIAR scientists working in three different crop areas, including one specifically in semi-arid agriculture.[67] Thus it is that the comparative politics of East African agricultural development are paradoxical. But, unfortunately, such a paradox includes a very sad tale of a country that promotes equity at the expense of national self-reliance and overall technical development.

CHAPTER 6

THE LIMITATIONS OF POLITICAL
VISION IN AN AGE OF TECHNOLOGY

THERE ARE PEOPLE hungry in Africa. The famine that currently grips the continent includes so many countries, and affects such a significant segment of the population of each, that it is almost of unimaginable proportions. The famine of the eighties embraces twenty-four countries, will cost close to two billion dollars to control, and has disrupted the lives of two hundred million people. A famine of such magnitude, like the plagues of the Middle Ages or the possibility of nuclear war today, is the kind of debacle that suggests the potential for either complete desolation or the apocalypse. It is as though we have stepped out of time and space when we confront the implications of such a set of circumstances. The reality is so devastating, the needs so overwhelming, that the scale and magnitude of the crisis itself seems to dictate the terms upon which a resolution will take place.

This is a delusion. The terms upon which a resolution to the crisis will take place are deeply rooted in a social, economic, political, and technological context that preceded the onset of the current famine, that mediates relief efforts, and that will remain in place long after the final distribution of food aid. The context that caused the crisis is not itself remedied by it. In examining the history of recent agricultural development in Kenya and Tanzania, we have learned about this larger context—how political institutions that are the major actors in the process of African agricultural development impede or accelerate necessary technical change; how technology impacts upon their goals and programs; and whether this impact assists in economic development and makes for worthy political and social change. These are extremely important relationships to be understood by African countries and those who assist them in their pursuit of agricultural change. Societies able to master technology and develop their agricultural sectors survive drought and emerge from periods of food shortage relatively unscathed; those with underdeveloped agricultural sectors become caught in a cycle of food deficits and establish a long-term dependence upon external sources of food. Will national and international policymakers choose strategies of development that result in feast or famine? Stated this boldly, the choice appears obvious, but the political and technical contexts in which such a decision is made obscure the stark discrepancies in outcome. In this chapter I will revisit those contexts and reconsider the lessons of East African agricultural development.

The Impact of Politics upon Technology

Agricultural development is a process of economic change, the success of which is dependent upon the ability of political institutions to mobilize technical resources. Politics is not necessarily a constraint or a facilitators of successful technology development and diffusion. Success depends very much on the ways in which particular organizational or state strategies complement or conflict with the requirements of technology development and adoption.

Traditional multilateral development assistance is carried out by international institutions of broad constituencies, ambitious world order goals, and extensive institutional development. Organizations like the FAO, the ILO, and the World Bank are universalistic in membership, globalistic in world order orientation, and highly bureaucratic. This means that each agency appeals to a very large constituency in order to launch new programs or maintain old ones. They rely on industrial countries for financial support and Third world countries for interest in and receptivity to the programs they carry out. They attempt to bridge the differences between these two sets of states with broadly defined goals and wide-ranging programs. Each agency is also responsible for a world order mandate of a special economic or technical purpose. As a consequence of appealing to a large constituency with diverse interests, and of attempting to remain active in the direct pursuit of world order as well as development assistance, the institutional structures of international development assistance have grown to mammoth proportions.

In such an assistance context technology becomes a political football, used to appeal to new constituencies or lure back the old, attached to world order ideals concerning the future of peace and harmony in the international system, and placed on the cutting edge of internal bureaucratic politics and institutional expansion. This is not to say that valuable technical programs are never launched in the context of traditional assistance. They are, and they have been, but they get lost in the institutional maze of trying to please all constituencies, globalizing national development programs, and fighting insiders' bureaucratic battles. This is what has happened to agricultural mechanization. The possible technology choices and avenues of technical development that might have been pursued in respect to the diverse needs of Third World agricultural change were attenuated by the political orientation of the agencies themselves. Agricultural mechanization became a captive of its political environment. Agencies were unable to cooperate in the design of a new technology or in the formation of a technical consensus on the utilization of the old. In the national context, this lack of consensus resulted in competitive international projects with little advance planning or follow-up. This magnified the already serious resource scarcity of East African countries.

If international agencies had chosen to cooperate in the development and execution of agricultural mechanization, they might have overcome these constraints to successful technical innovation. This is the alternative model of assistance that the international agricultural research regime, the CGIAR, represents. Each member organization or state continues to pursue highly individualized goals in a variety of other areas but chooses to jointly support the funding and review of international agricultural research and to informally cooperate in the field in the implementation of national research and technology diffusion projects. In order to develop such a technical focus, the constituency to which the regime addresses itself is small, the world order concerns remain limited to the construction of a technical regime, and institutional development and expansion are foregone. In comparison with traditional development assistance, the arrangement is highly elitist in political orientation. It does not attempt to appeal to all states or to develop the Third World as a whole. It is rooted in the work and programmatic practices of private foundations, which were able to make long-term commitments to very narrowly defined areas of development concern. These are the politics of successful technology development and diffusion.

Can the UN's system of multilateral assistance reform itself, and along with powerful bilateral actors and voluntary agencies begin to create other such technical regimes? The institutional and political momentum of several decades of a highly fragmented, universalistic structure of aid will be difficult to reroute. The role of economic development in the politics of international world order needs to be reconsidered by the international community as a whole for any massive reform to be implemented. There is no constituency for such international change. More likely is the possibility that the kind of technical vision for which the Rockefeller Foundation was responsible in the case of agricultural research will emerge in another technical area. Perhaps it will be fostered in a technical division or department within the UN behemoth, or, as was the case for agricultural research, given support by a small-scale institutional pioneer of whom little note is taken, until a terribly successful technology again presents the assistance system with a challenge and a choice. The serendipity of such a scenario does not bode well for any systematic reform of the structure of international aid.

Just as the universalism of traditional international assistance agencies impelled the definition of a political orientation of broad constituencies and massive institutional development, so the egalitarianism of Tanzanian socialism led it to strike out in a similar political direction. Tanzanian state building is a politics of broad participation and service. Ujamaa literally translated means familyhood, and the social notion of family-hood is very close to the political idea of fraternity. For Tanzania, like many other socialist states, the definition of such a communitarian perspective results in an interest in radical economic equity. Communal modes of property ownership and agricultural cultivation are created on the premise that public property assures social justice. Institutional development, as a consequence, must be extensive, and the power to penetrate society and alter the social relations of production inherited from colonialism must be well developed.

This strategy of state building makes the successful introduction and adoption of new technology extremely difficult. This is not because technology is given ideological importance; this happens in almost all national as well as international development contexts. The difficulty lies not in the presence of ideology per se or in the pursuit of political goals but rather in the highly diffused investment pattern and broadly defined technology transfer policy that follows from such socialist objectives. To appeal to a large constituency is to invest resources in a variety of economic environments simultaneously. To use technical resources to massively change the social relations of production across the nation as a whole and to extend political institutions at the same time is to pursue a technology transfer program of herculean proportions. This would not pose a problem for Tanzania, or any other socialist state, if there were a limitless supply of economic and technical resources, on the one hand, and an extensive system of technical support on the other. Tanzania has neither. Trying to reach everyone at once may mean reaching no one at all.

The legacy of colonialism aggravated the costs of the socialist, and accentuated the benefits of the capitalist strategy. Socialist states are more frequently at odds with their colonial past than are capitalist states. Eager to reject and reverse the patterns of economic development and social change that left some segments of society better off than others, socialist states do not build upon the sectoral and regional development infrastructure that is in place at independence. When the resource investments were extremely limited to begin with, as was the case in Tanzania, the development loss in respect to potential national income and agricultural productivity is even greater. Kenya maximized the possibility that its postindependence technology transfer efforts would be successful by investing its own development resources in the sectors and regions that the colonial state had supported. The cumulative impact of decades of investment in the White Highlands resulted in a network that fully supported the much less ambitious technology projects of the new state.

Thus, the constraints of technical support systems in largely agricultural, largely underdeveloped economies work in favor of a state-building strategy that limits its objectives, narrows its constituency, and concentrates the investment of scarce resources. Capitalist states, like Kenya, accept the social status quo in respect to the basic structure of the social relations of production, and need not, as a consequence, develop the central institutions of the state in as elaborate or extensive a fashion as socialist states. Much like international technical regimes, capitalist states do not concern themselves with social justice and thus do not diffuse the investment of development resources. The technology projects that they support are much less ambitious and thus more likely to fit the contours of the economic and technical environment into which the new technology is introduced. Capitalist states are no less political than socialist ones, but their politics are much more elitist socially and support a political economy of highly concentrated resource investment.

Finally, in respect to the impact of the organization of national politics on the introduction of new technology, the highly elitist approach of the capitalist state, in comparison with the greater egalitarianism of the socialist state, is more conducive to the support of the development of a technical elite. In some respects, this too has its roots in the period preceding the accomplishment of political independence. The available technical elite—or more accurately, the literate populations that might be inducted into higher education and training for the creation of a technical elite—was frequently from regions of the country that had benefited most from colonialism. Tanzania wished to deemphasize the importance of such groups, while Kenya was interested in their further development. This is not, however, only a matter of the colonial legacy. Tanzania's socialism, which is populist in spirit, is not at all comfortable with the establishment of a community of scientists or technical experts. Both states are eager to keep the development of a technical elite from becoming an independent base for the making of important policy decisions. But this is only an issue of ethnic politics in Kenya—the state can live with one type of technical elite, but not another—while in Tanzania the development of a such an elite appears to be seen as mutually exclusive of the political control of policy by the party and government administration. On top of this, the long-term commitment that must be made to such a community and the uncertainty of potential development outcomes is something a state impatient to reach the average peasant cannot easily countenance.

The impact of politics upon technical innovation is not foreordained by any necessary complementarity or contradiction between these two forces of developmental change and modernization. Clearly, some types of politics work better than others to foster technology change and agricultural development. Nevertheless, the absolute tradeoffs between technical success and overall social or international welfare are difficult to make. Egalitarianism taken too far can result in a lack of significant technical development and thus no significant agricultural change. Whether the locus of such a strategy is national or international, the outcome in respect to development policy robs African countries of a future of food self-sufficiency and national self-reliance. Elitism taken too far, while preserving the overall economic power of international and national food sectors, can disenfranchise large segments of Third World societies and fail to benefit those who find themselves on the bottom of the economic ladder. Who best feeds the hungry? In Africa today it is difficult not to conclude that while the creation of technical and economic capability may not be enough to assure that food will be distributed in a socially just manner, without those capabilities, there is very little to distribute, and a justice of only questionable merit.

The Impact of Technology on Politics

Technology is a special developmental resource, offering political institutions the power to redefine the basic contours of the economic, social, and institutional contexts in which they operate. The ability of institutions to exploit those opportunities and master the independent power of this resource depends very much on how the particular properties of individual technologies complement or conflict with organizational and state strategies of institutional change.

Agricultural research for the improvement of seed technology was a promising avenue of international cooperation for a variety of reasons. To begin with, at the point at which the CGIAR was founded, the technology had just established itself as an extremely successful instrument for the dramatic improvement of Third World food sectors. It quite literally basked in the light of international acclaim and attention. The scope of the technical success itself provided considerable momentum for the creation of the new regime. A second and no less important factor was the technical consensus that characterized this area of technical development. There was widespread international agreement on what should and what could be done to further the development of the technology and increase its impact upon Third World food agriculture. The existence of a technology paradigm set out a framework within which a community of researchers were able to collectively address a common problem. This paradigm cut across national, regional, and institutional boundaries and embraced many ecologies and physical environments, thus providing a strong international technical basis upon which institutions could cooperate. It was also significant that this was an area of technology development that did not challenge the work or the markets of any major multinational corporations. Innovation in this area did not entail any short-term redefinitions of the international social relations of production, and thus it did not challenge the status quo in respect to the international economic balance of power.

In comparison, an experience of considerable technology failure, a technical community in conflict with itself, and an international marketplace of big business competition characterized the technical area of agricultural mechanization. The tractor has been a spectacularly successful technology in the context of highly industrialized agriculture. No one would argue with its effectiveness in revolutionizing American food production at the turn of the century. However, in the context of the Third World, and more explicitly, the experience of international aid, there have been as many failures as successes. Tractors that were never effectively transferred, instead of increasing food production, slowly rust in peasant fields. Further, in some instances, the technology transfer resulted in the massive disenfranchisement of small-scale holders, increasing the power of landlords and large-scale holders at the expense of the welfare of the average cultivator. This is a story of limited technology success at best. At the same time, there have been no spectacular instances of an intermediate technology launching agricultural change and increasing welfare. In neither case—tractors or small-scale technology—was there the kind of technology success that might have galvanized interstate or interagency cooperation. Not surprisingly, there was also a marked lack of technical consensus on the subject of agricultural mechanization. The question of what should be and what needs to be done was up for grabs. The technical in-fighting among experts was as serious as the political battles across and within agencies. There was no paradigm of technology development or adoption, no agreement on whether large-scale or small-scale technology was best suited to peasant farmers. Finally, agricultural mechanization is an area of technology development in which there are major private actors with big stakes in the direction of technical change. If international agencies were to establish a new mode of international cooperation in the area of agricultural mechanization, they would certainly have to reckon with these actors.

The relatively greater success of assistance in the area of improved seed technology, compared with programs of agricultural mechanization, was only in part a matter of more astute organizational politics. The international regime was blessed with a technology that easily facilitated international cooperation and the success of the projects it sponsored. In contrast, the more traditional development assistance program struggled with a technology which itself accentuated the fragmentation of the institutional structure of assistance and the problems such a structure presents. The individual characteristics of the technologies in respect to a variety of factors offered or denied greater prospects for increasing institutional authority and legitimacy. While it was the political actors themselves who identified and acted upon the prospects technical innovation represented, the technology, nevertheless, imposed a kind of technical logic upon the institutions that utilized it.

Technology has imposed its own design upon national as well as international institutional development. This is most dramatically demonstrated in the case of the introduction of the tractor into peasant farming systems. States of all ideological and political stripes have identified the tractor as a technology of considerable independent power and have substituted it for institutional power that they either lacked or were unwilling to use. The tractor offers the state a number of opportunities for social and political change. It is able to literally restructure the physical environment in a major way and, thus, alter the layout of peasant farming systems. It operates best on large-scale holdings, serving as a justification for major changes in the scale of the organization of production. It is able to release the farmer and his family from a major expense of labor, and in this way serves as an inducement to changes which the state hopes to introduce along with the technology. And, finally, it can be utilized by the state to accomplish these tasks without actually being transferred into the hands and households of independent and autonomous peasant cultivators.

The real political drama of tractorization, however, lies in the contradiction between technical potential or promise and actual impact. For while the tractor does indeed offer all of these capabilities, it requires certain supports as well. To survive economically, the tractor needs highly profitable crops to cultivate, or extensive acreage of less-profitable agricultural goods. It is a capital-intensive technology, and one of the requirements of its adoption is capital. To survive in a technical respect, the tractor needs extensive institutional and infrastructural support. Either the state or the farming community must provide the necessary technical expertise, transportation, credit, repair and maintenence, and other such services. This dependence upon a large-scale context of supportive institutional services and functions makes the potential economic power of the tractor very difficult to mobilize in unindustrialized agricultural settings.

The utilization of the technology to restructure rural society is a highly problematic endeavor for states without the necessary system of support. It is not enough to have a good system of repair and maintenance but no marketable crops; not enough to have agricultural credit, but no gasoline stations; not enough to have an adequate system of transport, but no technical expertise. If there were one magic key to the production of a system of technology support, the problems of transferring the tractor into Third World farming systems would have been solved long ago. But there is no such key. There is no necessary complementarity among the various elements of such a system. Opening the door to a successful credit program or establishing a system of transport does not mean that trained manpower or marketable crops will follow. And there appear to be no shortcuts to the creation of such a system of support. Concentrated and cumulative investment over time—months, years, decades—results in the kind of technical, economic, and institutional interconnections that make the successful introduction of the tractor and other such modern technologies possible.

At the same time, it is highly unlikely that states will switch from the use of the tractor to the introduction of smaller-scale technology. The utilization of the tractor has not increased the authority and the legitimacy of the state. In some cases, the technology has failed for lack of infrastructure, and in others, for lack of the right system of production. Often, peasant cultivators recognize the political intent behind the technical program and resist. Nevertheless, small-scale technology is not seen as a viable political alternative to the tractor. The introduction of the ox plow or improved hand tools is the introduction of a technology especially suited to the needs of small-scale holders. These are technologies that have little applicability for large-scale production and are not easily controlled by central authorities. The widespread transfer of small-scale mechanical technology would allow the peasant farmer to increase his production while remaining relatively independent of the state. Neither capitalist nor socialist states are eager to promote peasant power. The technical capabilities embedded in the technology itself are all wrong for states interested in the establishment of large-scale production, the centralization of power, and the greater dependency of peasant society. Small-scale mechanical technology simply does not advance the interests of African state builders—capitalist or socialist.

Finally, agricultural research and the development of improved varieties of seed also offer the state opportunities for social and political action, but they are more sharply delimited than the political actors themselves supposed. High-yielding varieties of new food crops make excellent tools to fight regional political battles, but they are not very powerful instruments of class politics or massive social change. Because they are confined to rain-fed agricultural regions, high-yielding varieties will inevitably accentuate regional discrepancies in economic and technical development. Governments interested in meeting the special needs of such regions will find the technology well suited to their political goals; those wishing to pursue regional equity have no other choice but to invest in the possibility of future research breakthroughs. But while the technology is highly sensitive to the ecological determinants of successful diffusion, scale of production is relatively unimportant. Thus it cannot easily mobilize peasants into villages or provide a strong technical undergirding for the development of a rural aristocracy. While it is not being used as such, the technology is, like intermediate forms of agricultural mechanization, ideally suited to the establishment of massive economic change among small-scale, independent producers.

The impact of technology upon politics is no more inevitable than that of politics upon technology. Technology does not introduce socialist values into nonsocialist societies, capitalist motives into noncapitalist contexts, cooperative instincts into conflictual circumstances. It does not operate behind the backs of political actors, ready to run roughshod over the institutions of the state or realign the organizational allegiances of assistance agencies. In the first instance, the impact of technology upon politics has very much to do with the ability of political actors to recognize the opportunities technologies offer. In the second instance, the cost of the requirements of successful technical development and diffusion must be met. The ability to exploit such opportunities for action is not the same as the ability to identify them. Technology does not carry any necessary political or social values, but it does carry structural proclivities. With a technical paradigm, the international support of technical development is more likely. Within a national context of adequate technical services, technical adoption is more successful. Technology does not simply offer power, it can impose or deny it, depending upon how it is treated by the actors who utilize it. It is, in this respect, that technology makes its impact upon politics.

Development Assistance

International development assistance is a system of resource transfer consisting of the collective institutional environments of international agencies and Third World states. It is a highly complex set of institutional relationships distilled into individual assistance projects. There is no central clearinghouse or governing board for the system as a whole, which imposes any but the most casual order upon the interaction. Plagued by a history of only minimal success, agency officials as well as national policymakers are eager to know what kind of reforms might be introduced to rationalize the relationship of agencies to states. The best answer to this question is that there is none.

The findings of this study indicate that project success is very much dependent upon the pursuit of limited goals by both states and organizations. Change in one institutional environment is not enough to make for project success. The most conclusive instance of successful technology transfer reviewed in the previous chapters took place in Kenya as a consequence of assistance provided by the seed technology regime. The most dramatic failure occurred in Tanzania as a result of the assistance projects of traditional multilateral aid. More inconclusive were the efforts of aid agencies to assist Kenya in the area of mechanization and the regime's attempt to introduce a program of maize improvement in Tanzania. What was most important in each of these cases was the way in which the goals and capabilities of assistance agencies overlapped with those of the state. The elitism that was common to the Green Revolution regime and Kenya's approach to development resulted in extensive success. The interaction of universalism and broad constituencies in mechanization assistance and radical equity in Tanzania made for disastrous technology transfer. The lack of overlap or complementarity between organizational and state approaches to development in the other two instances of technology transfer led to a mixture of economic success and failure.

What is particularly interesting about this conclusion is that it indicates that neither actor is able to dominate the other. It is certainly true that in some areas of assistance policy, one actor is able to control the other. This is the case in the provision of major loans to states by economic actors like the World Bank or the IMF. If they so choose, they can deny credit to states who do not adopt the recommended macroeconomic policies. Similarly, states are able to deny organizations access to regions of the country and internal institutions that they deem to be politically sensitive. While acknowledging these very important areas of interaction, to understand the day-to-day, mundane experience of the design and execution of assistance programs, it would probably be better to move beyond questions of who dominates whom. Certainly in order to understand why some projects succeed and others fail, it is a matter of institutional complementarity and contradiction, the overlap of basic political development principles or their conflict, and not the ability of either to determine the outcome in any unilateral respect.

Thus, reform in the system as a whole could only come about through change in both national and international policy. If international development assistance slowly disappears with the waning of this century, it will be because of the declining interest in both the developed and developing world. Each has been fortified with the belief that assistance does not work as well as it should because of the lack of commitment and resources of the other. The assumption that assistance is a simple matter of resource transfer has fueled this debate. But there is nothing simple about transferring resources in order to prompt greater development. In part it can be orchestrated, in part it cannot. Blaming one side or the other for a lack of will or for the concern with political as well as economic investments misses all significant points. Both actors must simultaneously attend to the way in which their institutional development can promote economic transformation.

In the case of technology transfer, technological constituencies must be found. This is not a simple matter of socialism versus capitalism for the state, though it may very much be a matter of regime creation for international organizations. In both cases, initial constituency commitments in respect to economic welfare must be limited. This does not mean an acceptance of the trickle-down theory of development, but the delay of broad equity or universal development. Tanzania need not give up on its interest in social relations of production that result in peasant communes, but simply on the expectation that a program of technology transfer can set down a technical structure for those relations rather immediately, and that the welfare needs of those communes can be quickly and adequately met. Similarly, international organizations cannot expect that, given the resources at their disposal, they can pursue multiple avenues of assistance in dozens of states and effectively accomplish global development. Narrower goals must be set and to do so political retrenchment is needed.

Tanzania has been much heralded as the one African state whose politics indicate real concern with the peasantry. The international community has been praised for its strong commitment to the eradication of Third World poverty. However, in the end, good will and good politics cannot pull Africa—or for that matter other very poor regions of the Third World—out of its economic malaise. The resources at the disposal of a state like Tanzania or available to international assistance agencies are simply too limited to make ambitious welfare concerns anything other than fantasy. There must be a technical vision to accompany the political one, or the brave welfare proclamations of the mid-twentieth century will be little more than elegant rhetoric. Famine is on Africa's doorstep; with a commitment to gradual, incremental, technical change, it will be kept there, while the preparations necessary for the feast to come begin.

NOTES

1. The Politics of Technology Development and Transfer

1. Yujiro Hayami and Vernon W. Ruttan, *Agricultural Development: An International Perspective* (Baltimore: Johns Hopkins University Press, 1971); Bruce F. Johnston and Peter Kilby, *Agriculture and Structural Transformation: Economic Strategies in Late-Developing Countries* (New York: Oxford University Press, 1975); Sterling Wortman and Ralph W. Cummings, Jr., *To Feed This World: The Challenge and the Strategy* (Baltimore: Johns Hopkins University Press, 1978).

2. Theodore W. Schultz, *Economic Crises in World Agriculture* (Ann Arbor: University of Michigan Press, 1965).

3. Hans P. Binswanger and Vernon W. Ruttan, *Induced Innovation: Technology, Institutions, and Development* (Baltimore: Johns Hopkins University Press, 1978); Hayami and Ruttan, *Agricultural Development*; Vernon W. Ruttan, "Technology Transfer, Institutional Transfer, and Induced Technical and Institutional Change in Agricultural Development," in Lloyd G. Reynolds, ed., *Agriculture in Development Theory* (New Haven: Yale University Press, 1975), pp. 165–191.

4. Johnston and Kilby, *Agriculture and Structural Transformation*; Wortman and Cummings, *To Feed This World*.

5. Alain de Janvry, *The Agrarian Question and Reformism in Latin America* (Baltimore: Johns Hopkins University Press, 1981); Francine R. Frankel, *India's Green Revolution: Economic Gains and Political Costs* (Princeton: Princeton University Press, 1971); Keith Griffin, *The Political Economy of Agrarian Change: An Essay on the Green Revolution* (Cambridge: Harvard University Press, 1974); UNRISD, *The Social and Economic Implications of Large-Scale Introduction of New Varieties of Foodgrain: Summary Conclusions of a Global Research Project* (Geneva: 1974); Montague Yudelman, Gavan Butler, and Ranadev Banerji, *Technology Change in Agriculture and Employment in Developing Countries* (Paris: OECD Development Center, 1971).

6. On irrigation, see Jacqueline A. Ashby, "Technology and Ecology: Implications for Innovative Research in Peasant Agriculture," *Rural Sociology* (Summer 1982), vol. 47, no.2; Robert V. Burke, "Green Revolution Technologies and Farm Class in Mexico," *Economic Development and Culture Change* (October 1979), vol. 28, no. 1; Arthur J. Dommen, "The Bamboo Tube Well: A Note on an Example of Indigenous Technology," *Economic Development and Culture*

Change (April 1975), vol. 23, no. 3; Richard Grabowski, "Induced Innovation, Green Revolution, and Income Distribution: Reply," *Economic Development and Culture Change* (October 1981), vol. 30, no. 1. On mechanization, see Iftikhar Ahmed, "The Green Revolution and Tractorisation: Their Mutual Relations and Socio-Economic Effects," *International Labour Review* (July-August 1976), vol. 114, no. 1; Keith Griffin, *The Political Economy of Agrarian Change*, pp. 53–54; Yudelman, Butler, and Banerji, *Technology Change in Agriculture and Employment*, p. 54.

7. UNRISD, *Social and Economic Implications*, p. ix.

8. Yujiro Hayami, review of Johnston and Kilby's *Agriculture and Structural Transformation*, in *Economic Development and Cultural Change* (October 1977), 26(1):179.

9. Keith Griffin, *The Political Economy of Agrarian Change*, p. 82.

10. These three categories of analysis owe much to the Green Revolution theorists and John P. McInerney, "The Technology of Rural Development," World Bank Staff Working Paper No. 295 (Washington, D.C.: 1978).

11. Again, this discussion is dependent upon my interpretation of the Green Revolution literature and Nicolas Jequier, *Appropriate Technology: Problems and Promises* (Paris: OECD Development Studies Center, 1976); B. R. Williams, *Science and Technology in Economic Growth* (New York: Wiley, 1973).

12. Charles Tilly, *The Formation of National States in Western Europe* (Princeton: Princeton University Press, 1975); Gianfranco Poggi, *The Development of the Modern State: A Sociological Introduction* (Stanford: Stanford University Press, 1978).

13. Michael F. Lofchie, *The State of the Nations: Constraints on Development in Independent Africa* (Berkeley: University of California Press, 1971).

14. Thomas M. Callaghy, *The State-Society Struggle: Zaire in Comparative Perspective* (New York: Columbia University Press, 1984); Robert H. Jackson and Carl G. Rosberg, *Personal Rule in Black Africa: Prince, Autocrat, Prophet, Tyrant* (Berkeley: University of California Press, 1982).

15. Robert E. Asher, "International Agencies and Economic Development: An Overview," in Leland M. Goodrich and David A. Kay, eds., *International Organization: Politics and Process* (Madison: University of Wisconsin Press, 1973), p. 244.

16. Edward W. Erickson and Daniel A. Sumner, "The UN and Economic Development," in Burton Yale Pines, ed., *A World Without a UN: What Would Happen if the United Nations Shut Down* (Washington, D.C.: Heritage Foundation, 1984), p. 20.

17. Barbara B. Crane and Jason L. Finkle, "Organizational Impediments to Development Assistance: The World Bank's Population Program," *World Politics* (July 1981), vol. 33, no. 4; Isebill v. Gruhn, "The UN Maze Confounds African Development," *International Organization* (Spring 1978), vol. 32, no. 2; W. R. Malinowski, "Centralization and Decentralization in the United Nations Eco-

nomic and Social Activities," *International Organization* (Summer 1962), vol. 16, no. 3.

2. Agricultural Mechanization and International Institutional Fragmentation

1. Gove Hambridge, *The Story of the FAO*, (New York: Van Nostrand, 1955), pp. 54–55.

2. On the continuing need for the establishment of international cooperation in this area, see Raymond F. Hopkins and Donald J. Puchala, *Global Food Interdependence: A Challenge to American Foreign Policy* (New York: Columbia University Press, 1980).

3. Joseph M. Jones, *The United Nations at Work* (Oxford: Pergamon Press, 1965), p. 40.

4. FAO, Director General, *The Work of the FAO* (WOF) *1956–57* (Rome: FAO, 1957), p. 82; *WOF 1966–67* (Rome: FAO, 1967), p. 1.

5. FAO, Director General, *Programme of Work and Budget* (PWB), *1976–77* (Rome: 1976), pp. li, lvii; FAO, Director General, *WOF, 1966–67*, pp. 5, 234.

6. Hernan Santa Cruz, *FAO's Role in Rural Welfare* (Rome: FAO, 1959).

7. FAO, Director General, *WOF, 1956–57*, pp. 13–14; *WOF 1964–65*, pp. 18–19; *PWB 1976–77*, pp. 123–125.

8. H. J. Von Hulst, Agricultural Engineering Service, "Closing Statement," in FAO, *The Effects of Farm Mechanization on Production and Employment* (Rome: 1975), pp. 385–387.

9. FAO, *Report to the Government of Ethiopia on Small Agricultural Implements* (Rome: FAO, 1953), and *Report to the Government of Afghanistan on Small Agricultural Implements and Farm Tools* (Rome: FAO, 1953).

10. FAO, *Considerations and Procedures for the Successful Introduction of Farm Mechanization*, (Rome: FAO, 1954), pp. 9–10.

11. Harmut Von Hulst, "The Role of Farm Mechanization in Developing Countries," *Proceedings of a Workshop on Farm Equipment Innovations for Agricultural Development and Rural Industrialization*, Occasional Paper No. 16 (Nairobi: Institute for Development Studies, University of Nairobi, 1975), pp. 56–67.

12. K. C. Abercrombie, "Agricultural Mechanization and Employment in Developing Countries," in FAO, *The Effects of Farm Mechanization*, pp. 35–49.

13. G. McRobie, "An Approach for Appropriate Technology," in R. J. Congdon, ed., *Lectures on Socially Appropriate Technology* (Technische Hogesdevol, Netherlands: International Cooperation Activities, 1975), p. 19.

14. M. M. Hoda, "India's Experience and the Gandhian Tradition," in Nicholas Jequier, ed., *Appropriate Technology: Problems and Promises* (Paris: OECD Development Center, 1976), pp. 144–155.

15. E. F. Schumacher, *Small is Beautiful: Economics as if People Mattered* (New York: Harper Torchbooks, 1973); E. F. Schumacher and Geraldine Kline, "A Plea for Intermediate Technology," *Ceres* (May–June 1968), vol. 1, no. 3; Nicholas Wade, "E. F. Schumacher: Cutting Technology Down to Size," *Science,* July 19, 1975.

16. E. F. Schumacher and G. McRobie, "Intermediate Technology and Its Administrative Implications," *Journal of Administration Overseas* (April 1969), vol. 8, no. 2.

17. ITDG, *Annual Reports, 1970–1975; How the Intermediate Technology Development Group Promotes Appropriate Technology* (1975); *A Summary of Field Experience and Capability* (1976); E. F. Schumacher, "The Work of the Intermediate Technology Development Group in Africa," in ILO, *Employment in Africa: Some Critical Issues* (Geneva: 1973), pp. 131–150.

18. See Ernst B. Haas, *Beyond the Nation-State: Functionalism and International Organization* (Stanford: Stanford University Press, 1964), for the authoritative evaluation of the ILO's standard-setting operations.

19. Robert W. Cox, "ILO: Limited Monarchy," in Robert W. Cox and Harold K. Jacobson, eds., *The Anatomy of Influence* (New Haven: Yale University Press, 1973), p. 105.

20. Richard S. Roberts, Jr., *Economic Development Human Skills, and Technical Assistance* (Geneva: Librairie E. Droz, 1962), pp. 35–36.

21. International Labour Conference, 53d Session, *Report of the Director General: The World Employment Program* (Geneva: ILO, 1969); David Morse, "The World Employment Program," *International Labour Review* (June 1968), vol. 97, no. 6.

22. Tripartite World Conference on Employment, Income Distribution, Social Progress, and the International Division of Labour, *Report of the Director General: Employment, Growth, and Basic Needs,* (Geneva: ILO, 1976), p. 152.

23. Keith Marsden, "Towards a Synthesis of Economic Growth and Social Justice," *International Labour Review* (November 1969), vol. 100, no. 11 and "Progessive Technologies for Developing Countries," *International Labour Review* (May 1970), vol. 101, no. 5.

24. Iftikar Ahmed, "The Green Revolution and Tractorisation: Their Mutual Relations and Socio-Economic Effects," *International Labour Review* (July–August 1976), vol. 114, no. 1.

25. Fernando Cededa Ulloa, "Columbia and the ILO," *The Impact of International Organizations on Legal and Institutional Change in the Developing Countries* (New York: International Legal Center, 1977).

26. World Bank, *Annual Report, 1974,* p. 137; *1978,* p. 179.

27. Edward S. Mason and Robert E. Asher, *The World Bank Since Bretton Woods* (Washington, D.C.: Brookings Institution, 1973), pp. 711, 833.

28. World Bank, *Annual Report, 1978,* pp. 176–177.

29. J. H. Adler, "The World Bank's Concept of Development: An In-House Dogmengschichte," in Jagdish Bhagwati and Richard S. Eckaus, eds., *Development and Planning: Essays in Honor of Paul Rosenstein-Rodan* (Cambridge: MIT Press, 1973); Eugene R. Black, *The Diplomacy of Economic Development* (Cambridge: Harvard University Press, 1960).

30. Robert S. McNamara, *One Hundred Countries, Two Billion People: The Dimensions of Development*, (New York: Praeger, 1973).

31. Robert S. McNamara, *Address to the Board of Governors*, (Washington, D.C.: World Bank, 1973), pp. 6–7, 10.

32. World Bank, *Agricultural Credit Sector Policy Paper* (Washington, D.C.: 1975), Annex 10.

33. IBRD, Technical Operations Department, "Utilization and Maintenance of Agricultural Machinery," (Washington, D.C.: 1953), p. 7.

34. C. Peter Timmer, John W. Thomas, Louis T. Wells, and David Morawetz, "The Choice of Technology for Irrigation Tubewells in East Pakistan: Analysis of a Development Policy Decision," *The Choice of Technology in Developing Countries: Some Cautionary Tales* (Cambridge: Center for International Affairs, Harvard University, 1975).

35. Mason and Asher, *The World Bank Since Bretton Woods*, pp. 249–250.

36. World Bank, *Appropriate Technology in World Bank Activities*, (Washington, D.C.: 1976).

37. World Bank, internal memo, June 11, 1976.

3. The Mechanization of East African State Building

1. IBRD, *The Economic Development of Tanganyika* (Baltimore: Johns Hopkins University Press, 1961).

2. Julius K. Nyerere, *Freedom and Unity: A Selection from Writings and Speeches, 1952–1965* (Dar es Salaam: Oxford University Press, 1966), p. 165.

3. IBRD, *The Economic Development of Tanganyika*, p. 133.

4. D. G. R. Belshaw, "Agriculture Extension, Education, and Research," in G. K. Helleiner, ed., *Agricultural Planning in East Africa* (Nairobi: East African Publishing House, 1968), pp. 57–80.

5. On World Bank influence, see Dean E. McHenry, *Tanzania's Ujamaa Villages* (Berkeley: Institute of International Studies, University of California, 1979), pp. 16–17.

6. Nyerere, *Freedom and Unity*, pp. 182–184.

7. John F. Chant, "Agricultural Credit in Tanzania," Economic Research Bureau Paper No. 68.4, (Dar es Salaam: University College, 1968), p. 4.

8. The mechanization of Sukuma agriculture has been analyzed by S. E. Migot Adholla, "Power Differentiation and Resource Allocation: The Cooperative

Tractor Project in Maswa District," in Goran Hyden, ed., *Cooperatives in Tanzania: Problems in Organization Building* (Dar es Salaam: Tanzanian Publishing House, 1976), pp. 39–57; J. D. Heijen, "The Mechanized Block Cultivation Schemes in Mwanza Region, 1964–1969," Research Paper No. 9 (Dar es Salaam: Bureau of Resource Assessment and Land Use Planning, 1969); John C. de Wilde, *Experiences with Agricultural Development in Tropical Africa* Vol. 2: *The Case Studies* (Baltimore: Johns Hopkins University Press, 1967).

9. H. Mettrick, "Mechanization of Peasant Agriculture in East Africa," in A. H. Bunting, ed., *Change in Agriculture* (New York: Praeger, 1970), p. 558.

10. Uma Lele, *The Design of Rural Development: Lessons from Africa* (Baltimore: Johns Hopkins University Press, 1975), pp. 34–35.

11. Eric Clayton, "Mechanization and Employment in East African Agriculture," *International Labour Review* (April 1972), vol. 105, no. 4.

12. United Republic of Tanzania, Ministry of Economic Affairs and Development Planning, *Tanzanian Agriculture After The Arusha Declaration: a Report by Professor Rene Dumont*, (Dar es Salaam: 1969).

13. Hans Ruthenberg, *Agricultural Development in Tanganyika* (Berlin: Springer Verlage, 1964), p. 110.

14. Republic of Tanganyika, MOA, *Annual Report, 1961* (Dar es Salaam: 1961), p. 14.

15. Peter M. Landell-Mills, "On the Economic Appraisal of Agricultural Development Projects: The Tanzanian Village Settlement Schemes," in United Nations Economic Commission for Africa/FAO, *Agricultural Economics Bulletin for Africa* (Rome: 1966), p. 8.

16. T. H. Strong, *Report to the Government of Tanzania on Planning Agricultural Development* (Rome: FAO, 1967), p. 9.

17. Republic of Tanganyika, Central Statistical Bureau, *Census of Industrial Production in Tanganyika, 1961* (Dar es Salaam: 1964).

18. O. A. Sabry, *Report to the Government of Tanzania on Land Settlement* (Rome: FAO, 1969), p. 7.

19. United Republic of Tanzania, *Report of the Presidential Special Committee of Enquiry into Co-Operative Movement and Marketing Boards* (Dar es Salaam: 1966), pp. 71, 82.

20. Charles M. Downing, "Interim Report to the Government of Kenya on Agricultural Mechanization in Kenya" (Rome: FAO, 1969), p. 1.

21. C. M. Downing and J. R. Goldsack, "The Kenya Government Tractor Hire Service: An Interim Report" (Rome: FAO, 1969).

22. Jomo Kenyatta, *Facing Mount Kenya: The Tribal Life of the Kikuyu* (London: Secker and Warburg, 1938), p. 310.

23. Jomo Kenyatta, *Harambee! The Prime Minister of Kenya's Speeches, 1963–64* (Nairobi: Oxford University Press, 1964), p. 112.

24. Republic of Kenya, MOA, Rift Valley Province, *Narok District Annual*

Report, 1966 (Nairobi, 1966), p. 3; *1968* (Nairobi: 1968), p. 9; B. A. Stout and C. M. Downing, "Selective Employment of Labor and Machines for Agricultural Production," Monograph No. 3, (East Lansing: Michigan State University, Institute of International Agriculture, 1974), p. 18.

25. Downing and Goldsack, "The Kenya Government Tractor Hire Service," appendix.

26. *Ibid.*, p. 4.

27. Republic of Kenya, MOA, *Narok District Annual Report, 1968*, p. 5.

28. EAAFRO, *Minutes of the Ninth Meeting of the East African Specialist Committee on Agricultural Engineering*, September 18–19, 1973 (Arusha, Tanzania: 1973), p. 1.

29. Colin Leys, *Underdevelopment in Kenya: The Political Economy of Neo-Colonialism, 1964–1971* (Berkeley: University of California Press, 1975), p. 70.

30. Republic of Kenya, MOA, *Western Province Annual Report, 1967, 1968* (Nairobi: 1967, 1968).

31. Downing, "Interim Report to the Government of Kenya," p. 7.

32. Downing and Goldsack, "The Kenya Government Tractor Hire Service," p. 4.

33. Republic of Kenya, MOA, Central Province, *Nyeri District Annual Report, 1966; 1969; 1971* (Nairobi: 1966, 1969, 1971).

34. Republic of Kenya, MOA, THS, *Tractor Hire Service Annual Report and Evaluation, 1975/76* (Nairobi: 1976).

35. Republic of Kenya, MOA, Land and Farm Management Division, *South Nyanza District Annual Report, 1972; 1974; 1975* (Nairobi: 1972, 1974, 1975).

36. J. Heyer, "A Preliminary Report on Farm Surveys: Tractor and Ox- Cultivation in Makueni and Bungoma," in Sidney B. Westley and Bruce F. Johnston, eds., *Proceedings of a Workshop on Farm Equipment Innovations for Agricultural Development and Rural Industrialization*, Occasional paper No. 16 (Nairobi: Institute for Development Studies, University of Nairobi, 1975), p. 78.

37. P. N. Kiruthi, "Experiences with Kenya Government Tractor Hire Service," *9th Meeting, East African Specialist Committee on Agricultural Engineering*, September 18–19, 1973 (Arusha: EAAFRO, 1973).

38. Downing, "Interim Report to the Government of Kenya," p. 7.

39. IBRD/IDA, Permanent Mission in Eastern Africa, Agricultural Development Service, "Agricultural Mechanization in Eastern African Countries," Report No. 3 (Washington, D.C.: 1966), p. 4.

40. IBRD/IDA, Agricultural Projects Department, *Small Holder Agriculture Credit Project: Kenya* (Washington D.C.: 1967).

41. World Bank figures; Republic of Kenya, MOA *Western Province Annual Report, 1967, 1968.*

42. IBRD/IDA, Agricultural Projects Department, *Appraisal of Second Small Holder Agricultural Credit Project.* (Washington, D.C.: 1972), p. 8.

43. Republic of Kenya, MOA, Land and Farm Management Division, *Nyanza Province Annual Report, 1971* (Nairobi: 1971), p. 6.

44. See Eric Clayton, "Mechanization and Employment in East African Agriculture," in ILO, *Mechanization and Employment in Agriculture* (Geneva: 1973); Downing, "Interim Report to the Government of Kenya"; IBRD/IDA, *Appraisal of Second Small Holder Project*; B. S. White, Jr. and Charles M. Downing, "Some Problems in Financing Mechanization of Small Scale Agriculture," (Nairobi: MOA, 1969).

45. Downing, "Interim Report to the Government of Kenya," p. 3.

46. Republic of Kenya, MOA, *Narosurra Farm Mechanization Training Scheme: Progress Report, 1968* (Nairobi: MOA, 1968).

47. Republic of Kenya, *Report of the Working Party on Agricultural Inputs* (Nairobi: 1971), p. 36.

48. Government of Kenya, *Communal Farming Project: Annex 2.* (Nairobi: 1976).

49. Julius K. Nyerere, *Freedom and Socialism: A Selection from Writings and Speeches, 1965–1967* (London: Oxford University Press, 1968), pp. 231–250.

50. United Republic of Tanzania, *Second Five Year Plan for Economic and Social Development, 1969–1974* Vol. 1 (Dar es Salaam), p. 30.

51. *Ibid.*, pp. 27–28.

52. Nyerere, *Freedom and Socialism*, p. 320.

53. K. Marsden, "Report on Mission to Tanzania and Zambia," September 22, 1969–October 11, 1969 (Geneva: ILO, 1969).

54. *Ibid.*, p. 2.

55. ILO, World Employment Program internal interview, October 1976.

56. ILO, *Agricultural Engineering for the Subsistence Farmer: Tanzania/ Project Findings and Recommendations* (Geneva: 1974) p. 2.

57. P. K. Mujemula, "Summary of Work Done and Being Done by TAMTU," *7th Meeting, East African Special Committee on Agricultural Engineering*, February 1969 (Arusha: EAAFRO, 1969).

58. George MacPherson and Dudley Jackson, "Village Technology for Rural Development: Agricultural Innovation in Tanzania," *International Labour Review* (February 1975), vol. 111, no. 2.

59. George MacPherson, *First Steps in Village Mechanization* (Dar es Salaam: Tanzanian Publishing House, 1975).

60. F. K. Mujemula, "Small Scale Production of Agricultural Implements at TAMTU," *9th Meeting, East African Special Committee on Agricultural Engineering*, September 18–19, 1973. (Arusha: EAAFRO, 1973).

61. M. A. M. Maro, "Utilization of Farm Machinery and Allied Equipment on Some Selected Farms in Tanzania," East African Community Seminar on Cooperation in Agricultural Development, December 1974.

62. On villagization, see J. H. Proctor, ed., *Building Ujamaa Villages in Tan-*

zania (Dar es Salaam: Tanzanian Publishing House, 1975); R. Lawrence, L. Raikes, R. G. Saylor, and D. Warren, "Regional Planning in Tanzania: Some Institutional Problems," *Eastern Africa Journal of Rural Development* (1974), vol. 7, nos. 1 and 2.

63. James R. Sheffield, ed., *Education, Employment, Rural Development* (Nairobi: East African Publishing House, 1967), p. 4.

64. Government of Kenya, *Communal Farming Project.*

65. IBRD/IDA, "Agricultural Mechanization in Eastern African Countries," p. 2.

66. Republic of Kenya, *Report of the Working Party*, p. 24; Mettrick, "Mechanization of Peasant Agriculture," p. 561.

67. ILO, *Employment, Incomes, and Equality: A Strategy for Increasing Productive Employment in Kenya* (Geneva: 1972).

68. World Bank, *Kenya: Into the Second Decade* (Baltimore: Johns Hopkins University Press, 1975); see also Mitchell Harwitz, "On Improving the Lot of the Poorest: Economic Plans in Kenya," *The African Studies Review* (December 1978), vol. 21, no. 3.

69. UNDP/FAO, *Agricultural Equipment Improvement (on Small Farms)*, Project Proposal (Rome: FAO, 1976).

70. Bruce Johnston, *Report on Efforts to Promote Wider and More Efficient Use of Animal Draft Power in Kenya and Expanded Local Manufacture of Implements* (Stanford: Food Research Institute, 1983), pp. 6–8.

71. P. K. Gota, "Introductory Statement," in Westley and Johnston, *Proceedings of a Workshop on Farm Equipment*, pp. 6–16.

72. See S. D. Minto and P. Evan-Jones, *A Summary of the Proceedings and Recommendations of the Specialist Committee on Agricultural Engineering in East Africa, 1958–1969* (Nairobi: EAAFRO, 1969).

73. Institute for Development Studies, *Second Overall Evaluation of the Special Rural Development Programme*, Occasional Paper No. 12 (Nairobi: University of Nairobi, 1975); J. W. Leach, "The Kenya Special Rural Development Programme," *Journal of Administration Overseas* (April 1974), vol. 13, no. 2.

74. For a discussion of the Mwongozo Guidelines, see Rodger Yeager, *Tanzania: An African Experiment* (Boulder, Colo: Westview Press, 1982), pp. 61, 95.

75. *Africa Confidential*, vol. 15, no. 1.

76. Z. C. I. Makoni, "Trends in Rural Development: The Regional Development Fund," Ph.D. dissertation, (University College, Dar es Salaam, 1969).

77. United Republic of Tanzania, Secretariat for Decentralization, *Setting Up the New Regional Organization: RDD's Action Plan* (Dar es Salaam: 1972).

78. United Republic of Tanzania, *Second Five Year Plan*, p. 38.

79. IBRD General Agriculture Division, East African Projects Department, *Tanzanian Agricultural and Rural Development Sector Study*. Vol. 2: *Annex on Mechanization* (Washington, D.C.: 1974); David Vail, "Technology for Ujamaa

Village Development in Tanzania," Foreign and Comparative Studies/Eastern Africa No. 18 (Syracuse, N.Y.: Maxwell School of Citizenship and Public Affairs, 1975).

80. Maro "Utilization of Farm Machinery;" C. R. S. Muzo, *The Party: Essays on Tanu* (Dar es Salaam: Tanzanian Publishing House, 1976), p. 39.

81. John Connell, "Ujamaa Villages in Rural Tanzania," *Journal of Administration Overseas* (October 1972), vol. 11, no. 4.

82. Lele, *The Design of Rural Development*, pp. 114, 157.

83. *Ibid.*, p. 154.

84. International technical assistant, interview, Nairobi, February 1977.

85. FAO, *Assistance in Agricultural Mechanization—Tanzania: Mission Report* (Rome: 1975), p. 11.

86. J. M. Beeny, *Report to the United Republic of Tanzania on Agricultural Mechanization Study,* (Rome: FAO/UNDP, 1975), p. 15.

87. FAO, "A Note Prepared for Briefing the Minister of Agriculture," Dar es Salaam, February 28, 1977.

88. FAO/UNDP, *Assistance to the MOA with the Establishment and Operation of the Rufiji Agro-Mechanization Centre and Demonstration and Testing Farm* (Rome: 1975); FAO, *Organization and Operation of Tractor Hire and Field Maintenance Services with Supporting Workshops (Agro-Mechanization Centres) and Demonstration/Testing Farms* (Rome: 1975).

89. FAO/UNDP, *Assistance to the MOA*, p. 3.

90. Beeny, *Report to the United Republic of Tanzania*, p. 44.

91. Yeager, *Tanzania*, p. 64.

4. The Green Revolution: Technological Paradigms and International Cooperation

1. J. George Harrar and Sterling Wortman, "Expanding Food Production in Hungry Nations: The Promise, the Problems," in Clifford M. Hardin, ed., *Overcoming World Hunger* (Englewood Cliffs, N.J.: Prentice-Hall, 1969), pp. 166, 127–128.

2. Lester R. Brown, *Seeds of Change: The Green Revolution and Development in the 1970s* (New York: Praeger, 1970), p. 49.

3. Rockefeller Foundation, *Toward the Well-Being of Mankind: Fifty Years of the Rockefeller Foundation* (Garden City, N.Y.: Doubleday, 1964).

4. Raymond B. Fosdick, *The Story of the Rockefeller Foundation,* (New York: Harper and Row, 1952), pp. 279–288.

5. National Academy of Sciences, National Research Council, Commission on International Relations, *Supporting Papers: World Food and Nutrition Study* Vol. 2: *Agricultural Research Organization* (Washington, D.C.: NAS, 1977), p. 81.

6. Elvin C. Stakman, Richard Bradfield, and Paul C. Mangelsdorf, *Campaign Against Hunger* (Cambridge: Belknap Press, 1967), p. 10.

7. On leadership, see Nicholas Wade, "Green Revolution: Creator Still Quite Hopeful on World Food," *Science*, September 6, 1974.

8. Lowell Hardin and Norman R. Collins, "International Agricultural Research: Organizing Themes and Issues," *Agricultural Administration* (1974), vol. 1, no. 1.

9. Harrar and Wortman, "Expanding Food Production," pp. 91, 132.

10. Sterling Wortman, "Extending the Green Revolution," *World Development* (December 1973), vol. 1, no. 2.

11. Nicholas Wade, "International Agricultural Research," *Science*, May 9, 1975.

12. CGIAR, Review Committee, *Final Report* (Washington, D.C.: 1976), p. 51.

13. CGIAR, *International Research in Agriculture* (New York: 1974), p. 7; National Academy of Sciences, *Supporting Papers*, p. 73.

14. John K. Coulter, "The Consultative Group on International Agricultural Research," in Charles Weiss and Nicolas Jequier, eds., *Technology, Finance, and Development* (Lexington, Mass.: Lexington Books, 1984), p. 269.

15. John Gerard Ruggie, "International Responses to Technology: Concepts and Trends," *International Organization* (Summer 1975), 29(3):569.

16. Thomas S. Kuhn, *The Structure of Scientific Revolutions* (Chicago: University of Chicago Press, 1962), p. viii.

17. *Ibid.*, p. 68.

18. Wade, "Green Revolution," p. 844.

19. *Ibid.*

20. Keith Griffin, *The Political Economy of Agrarian Change: An Essay on the Green Revolution* (Cambridge: Harvard University Press, 1974); UNRISD, *The Social and Economic Implications of Large-Scale Introduction of New Varieties of Foodgrain: Summary Conclusions of a Global Research Project* (Geneva: 1974).

21. UNDP, "Lessening Dependence on Artificial Fertilizer," *Action* (March–April 1976), p. 4; "Green Revolution Now Stressing Help for Impoverished Farmers," *New York Times*, March 16, 1977, p.2.

22. Warren Boroson and Nick Eberstadt, "The International Food Policy Research Institute," *Rockefeller Foundation Illustrated* (September 1979), vol. 4, no. 3.

23. CGIAR/FAO, TAC, *Report of the Tac Quinquennial Review Mission to the International Institute of Tropical Agriculture* (Rome: 1978).

24. CGIAR, TAC, *Farming Systems Research at The International Agricultural Research Centers*, September 1978 (Rome: 1978), p. 1.

25. CGIAR, *Final Report*, p. vi.

26. Sterling Wortman, "Impact of International Research on the Performance and Objectives of National Systems," in *Resource Allocation and Productivity in National and International Agricultural Research* (Minneapolis: University of Minnesota Press, 1977), pp. 322–335.

27. CIMMYT, *Documents for Consultative Group, Budget* (El Batan, Mexico: 1975).

28. Lowell S. Hardin, "Food Foundation Agricultural Programs: Observations and Issues" (New York: Ford Foundation, 1974), pp. 6–7.

29. CIMMYT, *Review*, 1975 (El Batan, Mexico: 1975), pp. 22–23.

30. CGIAR, TAC, "Supplement to the Report on the TAC Quinquennial Review to CIMMYT" (Rome: 1976).

31. CGIAR, *Report of the Task Force on International Assistance for Strengthening National Agricultural Research* (Washington, D.C.: 1978), p. i.

32. CGIAR, *Constitution of the International Service for National Agricultural Research* (Rome: 1979).

33. International Agricultural Development Service, *Annual Reports* (New York: 1977, 1978).

5. East African Maize and the Comparative Politics of Technology Success

1. C. C. Wrigley, "Kenya: The Patterns of Economic Life, 1902–45," in Vincent Harlow and E. M. Chilver, eds., *History of East Africa* (London: Oxford University Press, 1965), p. 236.

2. Elspeth Huxley, *Settlers of Kenya* (Westport, Conn.: Greenwood Press, 1975), p. 25.

3. S. N. Hinga and Judith Heyer, "The Development of Large Farms," in Judith Heyer, J. K. Maitha, and W. M. Senga, eds., *Agricultural Development in Kenya: An Economic Assessment* (Nairobi: Oxford University Press, 1976), p. 227.

4. Marvin P. Miracle, *Maize in Tropical Africa* (Madison: University of Wisconsin Press, 1966), pp. 251–252; Wrigley, "Kenya," pp. 218–219.

5. R. S. Odingo, *The Kenya Highlands: Land Use and Agricultural Development* (Nairobi: East Africa Publishing House, 1971), p. 78.

6. J. K. Matheson and E. W. Bovill, *East African Agriculture* (London: Oxford University Press, 1950), pp. 56–63.

7. M. N. Harrison, "Maise Improvement in East Africa," in C. L. A. Leakey, ed., *Crop Improvement in East Africa* (Farmham Royal, England: Commonwealth Agricultural Bureau, 1970), pp. 27–36.

8. N. R. Fuggles-Couchman, *Agricultural Change in Tanganyika, 1945–1962,* (Stanford, Calif.: Food Research Institute, 1964), pp. 68–72.

9. Odingo, *The Kenya Highlands*, p. 34.

10. *Ibid.*, pp. xix–xx.

11. Wrigley, "Kenya," pp. 218–219.

12. William O. Jones, "Agricultural Trade Within Tropical Africa: Historical Background," in Robert H. Bates and Michael F. Lofchie, eds., *Agricultural Development in Africa: Issues of Public Policy* (New York: Praeger, 1980), pp. 27–28.

13. Rockefeller Foundation, Program in Agricultural Sciences, *Annual Report, 1959/60; 1960/61; 1962/63* (New York: Rockefeller Foundation).

14. Harrison, "Maize Improvement"; H. N. Harrison, "Major Problems Affecting Productivity of Maize," *Agricultural Research Priorities for Economic Development in Africa* Vol. 2: *Contributed Papers: Soil and Water Management; Crop Production and Projection* (Washington, D.C.: National Academy of Sciences, National Research Council, 1968).

15. National Research Council, *Supporting Papers: World Food and Nutrition Study*, Vol. 5 (Washington, D.C.: National Academy of Sciences, 1977), p. 71.

16. St. G. C. Cooper, *Agricultural Research in Tropical Africa* (Dar es Salaam: East African Literature Bureau, 1970).

17. Carey B. Singleton, Jr., *The Agricultural Economy of Tanganyika* (Washington, D. C.: U.S. Department of Agriculture, 1964), pp. 15, 54.

18. Republic of Tanganyika, MOA, *Annual Report, 1963* (Dar es Salaam: 1963), p. 1.

19. G. K. Helleiner, "The Composition of Agricultural Development Expenditures in Tanzania, 1963–64 to 1967–69," Economic Research Bureau Paper No. 68.11 (May 1968).

20. On staff shortages, see Ordway Starnes, *East African Cereal and Legume Institute: A Proposal*, Social and Research Council of Ministers, East African Community (January 1971); UNESCO, *United Republic of Tanzania: Higher Agricultural Education* (Paris: 1968).

21. A. K. Auckland, "The Role of Plant Breeding in Tanzania," in Jon Morris and Gerald Saylor, eds., *Technical Innovation and Farm Development in East Africa* (Kampala, Uganda: Makerere University, 1975), p. 18.

22. Ralph W. Cumming, *Report of a Feasibility Study on Cooperation Among Eastern African Countries in a Regional Cereal Crop Research Program* (New York: Rockefeller Foundation, 1968), p. 17.

23. *Ibid.*, p. 30.

24. IBRD, *The Economic Development of Kenya* (Baltimore: John Hopkins University Press, 1963), p. 85.

25. Judith Heyer, "The Marketing Systems," in Heyer, Maitha, and Senga, *Agricultural Development in Kenya*, p. 277.

26. L. H. Brown, *A National Cash Crop Policy for Kenya* (Nairobi: MOA, 1963), p. 9.

27. Harrison, "Maize Improvement," p. 36; USAID, "New Cereal Varieties: Corn in Kenya," *Kenya–Spring Review* (May 1969).

28. USAID, "New Cereal Varieties," p. 13; Republic of Kenya, *Report of the Working Party on Agricultural Inputs* (Nairobi: 1971), p. 19.

29. Republic of Kenya, MOA, Land and Farm Management Division, *Nyanza Province Annual Report, 1971* (Nairobi: 1971), p. 12.

30. USAID, "New Cereal Varieties," pp. 5–6.

31. A. Y. Allan and N. Nyeru, "Experience in Seed Production in Kenya," *Proceedings of the First FAO/SIDA Seminar of Improvement and Production of Field Food Crops for Plant Scientists for Africa and the Near East* (Rome: FAO, 1974).

32. John Gerhart, *The Diffusion of Hybrid Maize in Western Kenya* (El Batan Mexico: CIMMYT, 1975), p. 47.

33. W. M. Senga, "Kenya's Agricultural Sector," in Heyer, Maitha, and Senga, *Agricultural Development in Kenya*, p. 75.

34. Republic of Kenya, Ministry of Finance and Planning, Statistics Division, "A Comparison of the Industry of Cultivation on Large and Small Farms in Kenya," *Kenya Statistical Digest* (March 1972), vol. 10, no. 1, tables 2 and 3.

35. Harrison, "Maize Improvement," pp. 36–38.

36. Kenya National Agricultural Research Station, Maize Research Section, *Annual Report, 1966* (Kitale: 1966), appendix 1.

37. Republic of Kenya, *Report of the Select Committee on the Maize Industry* (Nairobi: 1973), p. 2.

38. Alexander Young Allan, "The Influence of Agronomic Factors on Maize Yields in Western Kenya with Special Reference to Time of Planting" Ph.D. dissertation, (University of East Africa, 1971).

39. Kenya National Agricultural Research Station, Maize Research Section, *Annual Report, 1972* (Kitale: MOA, 1972), p. 52.

40. FAO, *Report on the FAO/NORAD Seminar on Fertilizer Use Development* (Rome: 1973), pp. 97–99.

41. USAID, *A USAID-Sponsored Evaluation of the Vihiga Special Rural Development Project* (Washington, D.C.: 1974), p. 41.

42. Judith Heyer, Dunstan Ireri, and Jon Moris, *Rural Development in Kenya* (Nairobi: East African Publishing House, 1971), p. 59.

43. Colin Leys, *Underdevelopment in Kenya: The Political Economy of Neo-Colonialism, 1964–1971* (Berkeley: University of California Press, 1975), pp. 104–110.

44. Judith Heyer, "Who Benefits from the Price Increases?" *The Weekly Review* (Nairobi), February 8, 1975, pp. 26–28.

45. USAID, *Agricultural Research Needs of Tanzania* (Washington, D.C.: 1971).

46. United Republic of Tanzania, Ministry of Agriculture and Cooperatives, "Comments on the First Draft: USAID Report on Agricultural Research Needs of Tanzania," January 20, 1971. (Dar es Salaam: 1971).

47. Ford Foundation, *Tanzanian Program: Project Proposal* (New York: 1972).

48. Ford Foundation, inter-office memorandum, November 27, 1972.

49. United Republic of Tanzania, MOA, Division of Crop Development, *Preliminary Working Paper on Maize Research*, (Dar es Salaam: MOA, 1974).

50. Ford Foundation, Letter, August 1, 1977; IITA/USAID, *Tanzanian Agricultural Research Project, Annual Progress Report 1976 and Final Project Report*, (Dar es Salaam: 1976).

51. IITA/USAID, *Tanzania*, pp. 16–17.

52. *Ibid.*, p. 8.

53. IITA/USAID, *Tanzanian Agricultural Research Project, Annual Progress Report 1975* (Dar es Salaam: 1975), pp. 10–11.

54. Marketing Development Bureau, FAO/UNDP Project, MOA, "Costs and Methods of Subsidizing Fertilizer in Tanzania in 1975," (Dar es Salaam: 1975), table 5.

55. World Bank, General Agriculture Division, Eastern Africa Regional Office, *Appraisal of the National Maize Project,* (Nairobi: 1975).

56. L. P. Fortman, *An Evaluation of the Progress of the National Maize Project at the End of One Cropping Season in Morogoro and Arusha Regions* (Dar es Salaam: USAID, 1976).

57. Office of Technology Assessment, *Africa Tomorrow: Issues in Technology, Agriculture, and U.S. Foreign Aid* (Washington, D.C.: U.S. Congress, 1984), p. 20.

58. Zaki Ergas, "Why Did the Ujamaa Village Policy Fail? Towards A Global Analysis," *Journal of Modern African Studies* (September 1980), 18(3): 392–392.

59. Rodger Yeager, *Tanzania: An African Experiment* (Boulder, Colo.: Westview Press, 1982), pp. 37–38.

60. Office of Technology Assessment, *Africa Tomorrow,* p. 19.

61. Economist Intelligence Unit, *Tanzania and Mozambique, 1985,* nos. 1 and 2 (London: 1985).

62. Gerhart, *The Diffusion of Hybrid Maize,* p. 34.

63. Republic of Kenya, MOA, Land and Farm Management Division, *South Nyanza District Annual Report, 1975* (Nairobi: 1975), p. 28; *1973,* p. 54.

64. Republic of Kenya, MOA, *South Nyanza District Annual Report, 1974,* p. 48; *1975,* p. 57.

65. Kenya National Agricultural Research Station, *Annual Report, 1972.*

66. USAID, *Revision of the Non-Capital Project Paper: East African Food Crops Research,* (Arusha: 1975); USAID, *Report of East Africa Food Crops Research Project* (Dar es Salaam: 1975).

67. Office of Technology Assessment, *Africa Tomorrow,* p. 20.

INDEX

Abercrombie, K.D., 28, 29
Agricultural Engineering Service: 27, 28, 78
Agricultural mechanization: 4, 7, 41; role in world order goals, 23; and ITDG, 32; as vehicle for social reorganization, 49–53; and political struggle, 145; *see also* Kenya; Tanzania; Tractors
Agricultural research technological paradigm: 99–100, 136–39; *see also* International regime; Technological paradigm
Animal-drawn equipment: 32, 66; *see also* Ox
Appropriate technology: and ITDG, 29–32; and social justice, 62–72; *see also* Small-scale technology
Arusha Declaration: 63–64, 68; and Mwongozo Guidelines, 73
Asher, Robert, 18
Australia, 96

Barkan, Joel D., 55
Belgium, 96
Bellagio, Italy: meetings on international agricultural research cooperation, 92
Bretton Woods system, *see* IMF; World Bank

Canada, 96
Canadian International Development Research Center (IDRC): and Tanzanian agricultural research, 136
Cassava: 97; and Tanzanian emphasis on production, 136
Caterpillar Corporation, 78
Cattle, 111
Consultative Group on International Agricultural Research (CGIAR): contribution to world order, 90; institutional interests,
90–92; role in coordinating bilateral and multilateral aid, 92–97; organizational ideology, 93–94; organizational structure and budget, 94–97; as technological paradigm, 98–99, 102, 105–7, 145; and failure of technological paradigm, 103–4; and maize research, 116; focus on productivity, 131; and World Bank suppport for research, 134; *see also* International Regime; Maize; Technological paradigm
Chagga, 84
Chickpeas, 97
China, 64
CIAT, *see* International Center of Tropical Agriculture
CIMMYT, *see* International Maize and Wheat Improvement Center
Coffee research, 112, 113
Colombia, 115, 117
Colonial legacy: 1, 15, 82, 84; cereal culture, 110–12; effects upon agricultural systems in Kenya and Tanzania, 110–13, 119; and food sector in Kenya, 139; and agriculture, 147–48
Corn rust, 112
Cotton, 57–58, 112
Cowpeas, 97

Delamere, Lord, 111; and Njoro wheat research center, 115
Denmark, 96
Development Techniques, Ltd., 30
Dumont, Rene, 50

East African Agriculture and Forestry Research Organization (EAAFRO), 120
East African Major Cereals Project, 115
Ecuador 573 (maize variety), 115
Egypt, and CIMMYT PROGRAMS, 105